THE OTHER SIDE OF MILITARY LIFE

A Chaplain's Point of View

Raphael "Ray" P Landreville

www.TotalPublishingAndMedia.com

DEDICATION OF THE BOOK

This book is dedicated respectfully to all chaplains in the Armed Forces who gave a part of their lives to ensuring God has a place in the lives of our military personnel.

Raphael P. Landreville

ACKNOWLEDGEMENT

T he book *USS Shangri-La* proved invaluable as a reminder of events that characterized my tour on the ship and especially the sequence of happenings that brought order to my discussion. Especially appreciated was the mention of several religious events that played an important role in our lives onboard the *"Shang,"* such as the blessing of our chapel by Cardinal Kroll while we were under repair in the Naval Shipyards, Philadelphia, Pennsylvania, and the visit to the ship by students from Palma Majorca. My appreciation is also due to Jack Gillen and Joe Poquette, Marines I served with in the Far East and stateside whose friendship has lasted since our first meeting in Okinawa. After serving four years with the Marines, I believe the saying, "Once a Marine, always a Marine" applies to me one hundred percent.

TABLE OF CONTENTS

THE OTHER SIDE OF MILITARY LIFE

A Chaplain's Point of View

PREFACE

My intention for writing this book is to bring to light a factor about the military life that is almost always left unmentioned in books and stories about military life. This element of military life is the role the chaplain plays in the lives of our military personnel and their families.

Unfortunately, few are aware the presence of chaplains in the military has a history extending back to George Washington and the Revolutionary War when Washington insisted officers and men attend Sunday Worship services in each battalion. Prayer played a major role in the personal life of George Washington, especially during those moments of preparation for combat. As Commander and Chief of the Continental States, he insisted this country look to God for guidance and protection.

Regardless of the religion an individual practiced, Washington and our Founding Fathers took action to ensure there would be freedom to practice it according to their conscience. Those who have served also know that chaplains not only represent their individual spiritual traditions and practices but they also protect the religious rights of others ensuring that God has a part in the lives of military personnel, wherever they are stationed.

The activities of the military chaplain extend far beyond the sphere of religious practice. He is a part of the daily lives of military persona, I including their families. He is a counselor, an advocate, a teacher, and a member of their families participating in all phases of their lives. He is there at marriages and baptisms. It is the chaplain who rushes to the scene of an accident to administer the sacraments, and, unfortunately, it is the chaplain who brings the news that a spouse, parent, or child has died or was killed.

He is a confidant when personal problems are crushing and proper direction is absolutely necessary. He is a good listener when someone has a concern and needs to discuss it to find a reasonable resolution. This is especially true when the problem is very personal, perhaps embarrassing and not of a nature allowing for a discussion with members of a unit. Examples include notification a divorce is being considered, catching him by complete surprise. Suddenly he is aware of the impact this will have on him as he faces the loss of a woman he loves and the burden this will place on the children facing the loss of their dad and his relationship with them. Equally difficult to deal with is the notification a child has developed a deadly disease, or dropped out of school or is on drugs when dad is thousands of miles from home and unable to handle the problem personally.

Often the person most likely in a position to discuss, evaluate, and develop a workable solution is the chaplain. For most people, the Marine, sailor, or soldier is someone trained to fight for the protection of the country and is capable of accepting life's hurts without allowing them to affect his total person. However, like the rest of society, the destruction of a marriage is a disaster for military personnel; sickness or harm to their children tears their world apart; and unresolved financial problems keeps them awake at night and consumes their thoughts during the day. The person most able to assist and maintain confidentiality is the chaplain, whose position is greatly strengthened by the ability to bring God into the resolution process.

Since our Revolutionary War, recognition of God as the source of guidance and protection for our military and the need for chaplains has been a historical fact continuing to present day operations. The Chaplain Corps continues to be a vital element in military life.

The Other Side of Military Life is a story of the chaplain's unseen world of combat—often secret, at times pleasant, sometimes painful, but always a route to God's love and attention.

INTRODUCTION

As midday settled in, a cool breeze from Lake Superior moved across the quarry in south Marquette, Michigan—a welcome relief from the heat creeping into the middle 90's. About noon I received a frightening phone call telling me a young girl from our parish had drowned in a quarry a few miles from the Cathedral where I served as an Assistant Pastor. Attempts to find her had been unsuccessful.

I grabbed the sick call kit and hurried to the quarry. This is a swimming hole I know well, having grown up on Division Street in south Marquette. During summer vacations, I joined dozens of other neighborhood kids using it as a swimming pool. The quarry had very high walls serving as platform for jumping or diving. It was very deep, about 28 feet, with walls reaching straight down to the bottom. I don't recall accidents happening during the hours I spent swimming there, but I do recall it was a burial ground for cars needing to be disposed of. The water was always clean, and in the summer it was comfortably warm.

St. Peter Cathedral was two or three miles from the quarry, allowing me to reach the scene in a matter of minutes. Arriving at the quarry, I hurried toward a group of swimmers standing a few feet from the edge; some crying, others covering their faces with their hands, everyone stunned by the events taking place before them. Some stood quietly watching, unable to swim well enough to go in after the victim, a young girl.

Her dad had been working at a company located about the distance of two football fields from the quarry when a supervisor ran up to him, telling him his daughter was drowning. He had dropped his tools, dashed out of the building, and ran full speed to a ledge protruding from the wall of the quarry to the site where his daughter had last been seen swimming. Bystanders pointed to the spot they thought she could be found. Without stopping, he dove into the water, and seconds later he surfaced with his daughter. Swimmers helped him lift her out of the water and place her on a patch of grass.

Working to resuscitate her, he did everything he could, but his efforts failed. Exhausted, he took her in his arms, pressed her face against his, and cried. His hurt was unfathomable. I stood next to them, silent, witnessing this overwhelming expression of love and loss.

I knelt next to them, opened my sick call case, took out the holy oil, and anointed her forehead, praying for her and her dad. As he wrapped his arms around his daughter, her head tilted back, allowing her hair to flow downward lightly touching the ground. In a way it reminded me of the Pieta scene with the dead body of Jesus lying on the lap of His mother Mary while others stood silently stunned at the catastrophe they were witnessing.

Within minutes, an ambulance arrived. The medical team lifted the child from her father's arms, laid her on the grass next to him, and immediately began efforts to resuscitate her, but without success. After numerous attempts, they approached the child's father and told him further effort would have no positive results. He leaned over, picked her up carefully and held her once again. He stood there, silent, helpless, and kissed her for the last time. Tears rolling down his cheeks, he watched his daughter carefully placed in the ambulance. They told him they would take her to St. Mary's Hospital.

His hurt was so deep, I wondered if he would ever be able to accept the loss of his daughter. These feelings were shared and reflected in the faces of all those who witnessed the loss of this young girl.

I returned to the rectory, went to my room, and sat down on my chair, stunned. Nothing hurts deeper than to be present at the death of a beautiful young child and to watch her dad, tears streaming down his face, his arms wrapped around her, holding her tightly against his chest. I prayed the family would be given the strength to accept this tragedy, believing they would see her again in the arms of God waiting for their arrival in the next life.

Today, this scene is as vivid in my mind as the day it happened. Death, regardless of age, comes when it is least expected. Telling your family you love them should be a part of everyday life.

A few minutes after returning home, the phone rang; a sick call at the hospital. A parishioner was preparing for an operation and wanted to receive the Sacrament of the Sick before the procedure began. I picked up my sick call case and started for the door, realizing the priesthood makes us an important part of the lives of the people we serve.

The quarry tragedy would be repeated many times over during the following years but in other forms, locations, and age groups. But the hurt and sense of loss remained the same. I chose this incident to begin because it presents a side of the priesthood that is often unseen; yet it is an important role in the relationship between the priest and his parishioners. Thank God, most encounters reflect peoples' daily lives, like baptisms, marriages and school activities where happiness is shared.

However the life of a priest would not be complete was he not a participant in all areas of life, including tragedies.

Chapter 1
First Parish Appointment

After I had completed the years of preparation for the priesthood, I was ordained and assigned to parish work. I was fortunate my first assignment was to St. Francis de Sales Parish in Manistique, Michigan—a fairly large parish with a primary school that has eight grades, with nuns teaching all of the classes. Their competence level and commitment to a quality education for all of the students remains amazing. Although I visited the school every day, there was no need for me to teach religion, as the sisters covered the subject thoroughly. On occasion, I would bring in a copy of *Mad Magazine*—not a very religious publication, but the kids enjoyed the change. Visiting the students quickly became a rewarding experience. The kids were happy, excited, fully involved in a very active parish, a perfect parish to begin my priesthood.

Without a parish high school, our students attended the public high school, and religion classes were conducted once a week at a room in our grade school. There was no facility acceptable for our high school students in our CYO (Catholic Youth Organization) to gather socially. The Knights of Columbus had a building for their meetings, social events, and adult recreation. In an effort to assist, several days a week they allowed their facility to serve this purpose and added a pool table, music, and enough space for a dance floor. Crowds varied, but it remained an active club.

Some of us played basketball, and on one occasion we agreed to play a game against the CYO in Newberry, Michigan; an hour or so drive from Manistique. However, we had a small problem. There were not enough Catholic students who played basketball to have a fairly good-sized team. A number of the high school students using the KC recreational hall were not Catholic but were competent basketball players and spent time at the KC Hall. So, without baptizing them I drafted them into our CYO. We took the challenge from the Newberry

CYO and played the game on their court. Although there were no future NBA stars on either team, we managed to hold our own and lost by just a few points, blaming the loss on their home court advantage. We had a party after the game, made new friends, and returned home exhausted but anxious to do it again.

Dinner Guests

One evening when home alone I enjoyed a roast beef sandwich sliced from a roast prepared for the next day's dinner. A sandwich, a bowl of soup, and a piece of cake made an excellent meal. As I washed the dishes, there was a knock at the backdoor. I opened it and saw an elderly man ready to ask a favor. "Can I have something to eat? I'm really hungry."

"No problem," I answered and returned to the kitchen. Using the beef roast our housekeeper had prepared, I made a sandwich, wrapped it in wax paper, and gave it to him. He thanked me and left. I returned to the living room, picked up the daily paper, and sat down. Twenty minutes later, I heard someone knocking at the back door. When I answered it, another hungry visitor was asking for something to eat.

"No problem," I answered. I returned to the kitchen to carve another slice off the beef roast and made him a sandwich. The third time it happened, I realize I was "being had." When I returned to the kitchen, a glance at what was remaining of the roast told me I was in serious trouble with Linda, our housekeeper and cook.

Sure enough, when she returned home later in the evening, it took about ten seconds before I heard, "What did you do with the roast?" There was no place to hide, so I told her about the visitors who really enjoyed her cooking skills, as did I. Although she never did, she threatened to make me a part of the next roast.

St Francis Parish in Manistique proved to be a great parish. This Lake Michigan coastal city made fishing an easily accessible recreation, and the forests surrounding it proved outstanding for bird and deer hunting.

Starting a Mission Parish

About fifteen miles west of Manistique, on US Highway 2, there was a small community with some Catholic families who, at times, had difficulty getting to Mass on Sundays. This was especially true during the winter months when snowfalls made driving hazardous. The pastor suggested we assist them by forming a mission parish using a public meeting hall for Sunday services. We met with the families in the area and found them anxious to make it happen.

Two problems developed from almost the very beginning: one, the collection was light. To correct this matter, we began to have "bingo parties" on several evenings during the week. Participants of all or no faiths joined the fun and greatly improved the mission's financial status. The second problem concerned ensuring the building was open for the Sunday morning service. For the first four or five Sundays, the building manager was there early so Mass could start on time. Then, for two or three Sundays, he failed to open the building on time, so I would have to drive to his home and knock on his door, reminding him we needed to get into the building. His family would then hurry, drive to the hall, and open the doors. It was gradually apparent this "going to Mass" business was rather inconvenient. On the following Sunday I arrived at the mission to find the manager was not there again. I drove to his house to repeat the request. As I walked to the front door, I saw the keys to the building hanging on the door handle. Ultimately, this proved to be an acceptable solution. After my transfer to Marquette, my replacement, Father Richards, built a church formalizing the mission's presence in the area.

Ingenious Deer

In an incident on a deer-hunting trip, seven hunters formed a line along the edge of a field and began to walk into a thicket of trees, making noise to scare any deer in the area and chase them in the opposite direction. At a clearing on the opposite side of the woods, two hunters waited to get a shot at any buck hurrying into the clearing. A game warden was standing to the side of the clearing, watching the exhibition. Suddenly a buck, with antlers at least eight spicks, moved consciously into the clearing, looked around, and saw large log lying at the edge of field. He quickly moved to the log and squeezed under it as far as he could. The hunters entered the clearing, walked right past the deer, and continued their advance into the next thicket. When the danger had passed, the deer quickly returned to the forest and disappeared. At least in this case, the deer outsmarted the hunters.

Transfer to St. Peter's Cathedral, Marquette, Michigan

Two years after my assignment at St Francis, Manistique, I received a transfer to St. Peter's Cathedral in Marquette, Michigan where I spent the next four years. St Peter's was an active parish with both a grade and high school. Both schools had a full complement of sisters teaching all grades. They did a marvelous job of teaching scholastic classes and were the real instructors on the subject of religion. We had two assistants at the cathedral. Msgr. McKevitt, a pastor, insisted both of us take an active part in both school programs, so Fr. Tom Coleman and I taught religion classes in the primary school.

Students at the high school came from all the parishes in the city, so assistants from the other parishes taught religion classes at Catholic Central. The priest teaching religion amounted to confirming the instructions the sisters had already instilled in their classes. The schools operated with excellence benefiting from the expertise the sisters brought to the schools. We all knew the sisters were the best educated women in the country as they taught their subjects during the school year and spent their summers back in college increasing their knowledge and developing new skills.

I recall a time when the public high schools were participating in science fairs. Catholic Central had never taken part and received considerable criticism for their lack of interest in the program. In an effort to cooperate with the other schools, Catholic Central took part in the program. I learned some time after I left the parish that the school won a majority of the first place competitions. I do not know if they continued taking part in this program, but it was an excellent beginning.

St. Peter's had a large congregation, and, like any other parish with a school, parish work and total involvement in the schools absorbed our days. Scholastic efforts were the major function of the school systems, but athletics absorbed a lot of our time. I was the Athletic Director for both the primary and secondary schools. Our main sport was basketball, with a fairly good but less than great winning record. It was obvious the team had the necessary skills but was not totally comfortable handling the ball and running plays.

The students came from different schools, so there was a need to become familiar with other team members and develop plays adaptable to this diverse group. The basketball coach for Catholic Central and I discussed the situation and reached a decision. The students had to become proficient in the game long before they reached Catholic Central and there had to be a great deal of concentration on ball handling and working plays. They had to become so familiar with handling the ball it felt like a part of their bodies. By the time the students entered high school, there was insufficient time to get them to their best. The team was competent and competitive but needed to reach a higher skill level. They had to become saturated with the sport long before they reached their high school years.

So we started training the kids in the third grade, stressing ball handling, looking for players who are open, and learning to shoot the ball from various positions on the court. By the time they were in Catholic Central, they would have the skills needed to be a first class competitor. I left the city before our team had reached the level of play necessary to be a top contender. However, later on I learned the kids we trained in grade school won the state championship for their school's classification. It rings true practice make perfect.

Chapter 2
Enlisting in the US Navy

E nlisting in the Navy as a Catholic Chaplain followed a family tradition of serving in the Armed Forces. My dad served in the Army during WWI, and my older brother served in the Army during WWII. I also wanted to serve in the Armed Forces but selected the US Navy.

I discussed it numerous times with Father Matt Jodocy, a classmate who was secretary to the Bishop. Matt suggested I prepare a letter requesting the Bishop's approval to enlist in the Navy, and he suggested I prepare the request immediately, as the Bishop was leaving town the next day to attend a conference in Rome. Minutes later, I was at my desk composing my request. As soon as it was completed, I called Matt, and we drove to the post office, had it stamped, and Matt placed it on the Bishop's desk.

Fortunately, the Bishop read my request, approved it, and told me to take the necessary steps to enlist. The next day, I contacted the Navy and enlisted as a Navy Chaplain. A week or so later the Navy accepted my enlistment and directed me to take a physical examination at the Great Lakes Naval Center in Chicago, Illinois. I drove to Chicago, stayed overnight, and the next morning reported to the base for my physical.

The day was Wednesday; the time early afternoon. I entered a room about half the size of a football field. The walls were Navy gray, with twenty-foot ceilings. Groups of sailors were bent over their desks, engrossed in issues absorbing their attention. I joined a long line of men working their way toward a table where corpsmen were giving immunization shots.

Standing about ten feet or so behind the table, a corpsman was carefully poking holes in an orange. Although he seemed to exhibit confidence in this effort, I was less than excited about being one of his first victims. I was thinking, "Dear Lord, don't let me be his first victim." However, it appeared our Lord had more pressing matters at hand. When I reached the table, I found myself stretching out my arm to this "orange puncher." The muscle in my left arm stiffened, as I was sure he would make more than one attempt to locate the appropriate vein. As he grasped my left arm, he said, "Relax." I did and waited, certain my concern would be realized. I turned my head away from him, and to my surprise he administered the shots carefully and with little if any pain.

At the completion of the physical, I signed appropriate papers and left the facility happy to begin taking the preliminary steps to entering the Navy full time. The next step was attendance at the Navy Chaplain Training Command in Newport, Rhode Island. Knowing the next training program would begin in a month or so, I returned to the Cathedral in Marquette and continued my work at the parish. Around the first week of June, newly ordained priests were ready for assignment. The diocese was in the process of placing the newly ordained priests and reassigning other priests to parishes, an annual practice. Since I would leave the parish in a few weeks to enter the Navy, I was given a temporary assignment to assist in a parish in Ironwood, Michigan. My brother, also a priest, was stationed at a parish in the same town, allowing us to spend some time together before leaving the diocese.

Navy Chaplain Training Center at Newport, Rhode Island

Two months after my physical, I received a formal "Report to duty Notice." The orders directed me to report to the Chaplain Training Center at the Naval Station, Newport, Rhode Island. Knowing some history of the East Coast, the assignment was more than enthusiastically received. The orders gave me sufficient time to set my affairs in order and spend some time with my folks in Wausau, Wisconsin. As I prepared to leave, my dad reminded me he served in WWI and that my older brother served in the Pacific during WWII and that I was carrying out a family tradition. I told him I had a sense of pride following the family tradition, but I preferred to do so in the US Navy and was anxious to begin my tour.

Shortly after enlisting in the Navy Chaplain Corps, I received a letter from the Navy, accepting my enlistment and commissioning me a naval officer. Included with this notification were instructions that I would be assigned to a Naval Chaplain Training Program conducted at the Newport, Rhode Island Naval Training Command. Since this program is not in continuous operation, I would be notified to attend the next session. Around the same time, I received a letter from the Military Ordinariate, a separate diocese responsible for the priests and military personnel serving in the Armed Forces, welcoming me aboard. All Catholic chaplains serving in all the Armed Forces fall under its jurisdiction although the individual priest remains attached to his diocese of origin, in my case, the Diocese of Marquette, Michigan. Later in my tour, a Bishop from the Military Ordinariate would conduct the Sacrament of Confirmation for children of Marine and Army families stationed at bases located near each other in California's Mohave Desert.

Toward the end of August, I received orders to attend the Chaplain Training Program in Newport. Needless to say, I was anxious to make the trip and begin my military service.

Upon arriving and reporting in, I had to purchase uniforms. Fortunately, the uniform shop was prepared to suit up someone like me who arrived in civilian clothes without any gear that even resembled military attire. By the time classes began, I was in uniform, fully prepared to begin the training program.

Entering the Chaplain Training Program was a step into a brand new world. We left parish life with its self-regulated lifestyle into a world totally regulated by military authority, where schedules were tight and our days were planned from the time we awoke in the morning until we went to bed that night. Having spent twelve years in the seminary preparing for the priesthood, tight schedules and demands on my time were not a new experience. However, six years had passed since that way of life, so in a way I was re-experiencing a former life.

However, one of the biggest, and in many ways one of the most important, was living and working with Protestant ministers and a Jewish Rabbi in close everyday activities. I discovered that a number of the Protestant chaplains had never met a Catholic priest personally. It was interesting to discover that this inexperience had little if any influence on the relationships we developed over the weeks of training. Our interest and concerns centered on the demands made on us as we worked together, ensuring the religious needs of all military personnel and their families were met and protected. It became clear rapidly that we were all a part of bigger picture where the best interests of the troops determined our relationships and the way we performed our ministries.

Our school programs were designed to instruct us to perform the mission of the Navy Chaplaincy effectively stressing the four basic principles that would govern our work.

Four Major Responsibilities of Navy Chaplains

There is a basic understanding that chaplains selected for work in the Armed Forces are fully knowledgeable and competent in the doctrines and practices of the faith they represent. So the training program concentrates on methods best suited to delivering religious services, knowledge of the Naval and Marine operational structure, where we fit in the chain of command, and the need to be fully involved in the lives of the military personnel and their families.

Fundamental responsibilities of the chaplain are summarized as follows:

Provide religious ministry and support to those of their own faith: This function was our main focus and actually a continuation of the priesthood we lived prior to entering the Navy. The basic principles governing our lives while serving as parish priests would remain the same. Our mission continues to be caring for our personal spiritual fitness and the growth and maintenance of the faith for those to whom we would minister.

For the parish priest, the congregation, the church and school absorbs his life. Religious order priests live monastic lives taking vows of poverty, chastity, and obedience and are committed to accomplishing the purpose for which the order was established. For example, the Maryknoll Society is dedicated to working in foreign missions; others manage educational institutions or have a mission of caring for the sick and the poor. The military chaplain stands alone in the work he does and the circumstances in which he performs his priesthood. His parish could be a battalion of Marines or the crew of an aircraft carrier. Regardless of the size or location of the military unit to which he is assigned, at least 25% to 30% of them will be Catholic. On an aircraft carrier with a crew in excess of 5,000, the Catholic population will be at least 1,250, and when family members are included the numbers increase by the thousands, forming a very large parish.

Today there are over 1.4 million total military personnel on active duty. Of that number, almost 375,000 are Catholic. Since the chaplain also has responsibility for the military families another 800,000 are added to the number. Today there are 223 Catholic priests on active duty in the military. The total number of parishioners served by the chaplains is 1,175,000. If numbers mean anything, this number reveals that each Catholic chaplain in the Armed Forces has an average parish of 5,270 parishioners! To assist in meeting the needs of Catholics in the Service, civilian priests have been authorized to assist on military bases that lack the presence of a Catholic chaplain.

In our class, we had about thirteen new chaplains, four of whom were Catholic priests. Regardless of the administration governing our society or their attitude toward our faith as priests, we give our best effort to ensure the sacraments and matters of faith are administered as conveniently as possible under the circumstances in which we serve. In a way, for me, the Mass kit demonstrated the nature of the service we were always ready to give. The kit was a small suitcase-like satchel that holds the vestments and articles needed for the celebration of the Mass. It was a constant companion throughout our tours, allowing us to celebrate the Mass in any appropriate location—a chapel, hanger bay, or the hood of a jeep. It seemed to demonstrate that we will be with you, whenever and wherever you are.

Facilitate religious requirements of those of other faiths: This obligation is very serious, as it stems from the demands of the First Amendment. Although on every base to which I was assigned we had both Catholic and Protestant chaplains, there were occasions when the religious needs of a sailor or Marine were not served by either the Protestant or Catholic chaplain. Most often this would happen when someone has a serious personal problem and needed to resolve it—a marriage problem, help for a sick child, financial problems that have gotten out of hand, or a moral situation that called for understanding and encouragement to find and employ appropriate corrective action. When someone wishes to participate in religious services performed in a faith other than ours, every attempt is made to locate representatives of that faith and arrange for opportunities for the person to contact them and arrange for their participation. Although counseling non-Catholics took place, I do not recall being asked to locate a worship service not available on our base or ship chapel services.

Care for the religious service personnel and their families: Much like parish life, working with families quickly became a major part of my life as it is a major part of the lives of the military, and in many ways they were the most enjoyable hours spent during my tour. Baptisms, confirmation, religious education of the children, marriages and funerals, an invitation to dinner, or a visit to a home became rewarding experiences. In a way, I was becoming a part of the families. Relationships developed that were strong and personal, creating an atmosphere of trust and openness allowing a discussion of personal subjects when an outside opinion would be welcome. Occasionally a marriage problem would arise as extended separations made managing a household with children a very difficult task. Finances were worrisome, especially in the lower grades when purchasing household goods and recreation had to be regulated closely. The lives and activities of the children were the same as they were in civilian life—the same problems in school, keeping curfew, selecting companions with a sense of morality, and in a sense, surviving an existence involving changing schools every few years as transfers governed where and how long a billet lasted. Military children developed a characteristic resulting from their frequent transfers: they made friends quickly, an unconscious reaction knowing they did not have long periods of time to become an active part of their school or neighborhood.

Advising the command concerning religious and social issues: This responsibility involves the best interests of the military, the personnel, and their families. Items of concern included whether to allow a raffle to benefit the Navy League when some may believe gambling is sinful, or whether the complaints of some of the folks in the brig had any foundation or were just another attempt to disrupt an otherwise well managed operation. What was generally called for was a certainty that the religious programs carried out by the chaplains met the needs of those in our command. Fortunately, every command in which I served respected the work we did and ensured we received all the cooperation we needed to care effectively for the religious needs of those we served.

Living And Working With Ministers Of Different Religious

Taking place in an almost unconscious manner was an association with ministers of other religious faiths, including a rabbi. For the first time in most of our lives, Catholic priests lived together and participated in programs with Protestant ministers and a Jewish rabbi. In some ways, this was not a new experience. We had all known Protestant ministers and Jewish rabbis from our social activities while working in our parishes or teaching in a university.

What did seem a bit strange was realizing that, with one exception, we were all Christians. All the Protestants ministers were members of denominations with origins in the Catholic Church, yet in civilian life we lived in two different religious worlds that had little if any social contact. All this changed the first day we entered the Chaplain Training Program.

For the weeks that followed, we ate together, attended class together, participated in the same physical training exercises, and helped each other complete tasks requiring the cooperation of classmates. It didn't take long to realize our religious differences had no impact on the activities in which we were engaged. As the program extended, friendly relationships developed as we began to know each other and became familiar with our histories. I do not recall an incident where a difference in religious belief affected our training programs.

The Chaplain Training Program proved to be a valuable experience for all of us. We spent our hours learning about the Navy, the chaplaincy, and participating in physical exercises. Taking place in an almost unconscious manner was an association with ministers of other religious faiths, including a rabbi all of whom were friendly and respectful. We learned that we could work together for the good of those we served. In fact, later in my chaplaincy I met a Lutheran minister and his wife, and over the course of our service together, he became one of my best friends.

Since nearly all chaplains entered the service with little or no knowledge of naval or Marine operations it was paramount to ensure that we became familiar with their organizational structures, customs, procedures and other activities that are part of everyday navy life. The program was designed to make chaplains aware of their responsibility to ensure sailors and Marines were given the opportunity to practice their faith wherever they served, ashore or at sea.

There were limited physical training programs stressing the need to stay in shape. There were some required physical competencies that everyone had to meet. Everyone could swim but there was one exercise involving the need to do 15 push-ups that one of the chaplains was not able to do, although he gave it a good try. Eventually he managed to reach that number, although it took him a long time and left him totally exhausted. We also had marching formations that were performed acceptably, but none of us would have been accepted as members of a demonstration team.

Danko, a former submarine Warren Officer, managed our physical training programs. His instructions were always clear, but his greatest virtue was patience, for which he will always be remembered. One exercise consisted of learning some very basic terms referencing the structure of the ship. For instance, the front of the ship is known as the bow and the back of the ship is the stern; when facing the bow, the left side of the ship is port and the right side is starboard. Although not a momentous bit of information, it is absolutely vital aboard ship, where the terms are in constant use in every operation.

However, for many of the "airedales" pilots the bow of the ship was the "peaky" point and the stern was the "flat end." I suppose when landing an aircraft at 140 miles an hour, it doesn't make a great deal of difference what is the actual name of ship parts. What is really important is catching one of the four cables stretched across the flight deck, ensuring a safe landing. An exercise we watched but were not participants involved plugging a hole in the hull of the ship as water was rushing through it. We watched a crew take the appropriate action, which included grabbing everything in sight and stuffing it in the hole until the flow stopped. The result wasn't pretty, but the hole was plugged and the imaginary ship saved. In real life, failure to fill the hole would send the ship to the bottom—and the crew with it.

Submarine Cruise

A trip on a submarine probably was the most appreciated exercise. We boarded a submarine, a post WWII vessel, to practice several diving exercises. Touring the submarine, we became aware of the close quarters in which the crew lived. The passageways were narrow. It appeared every inch of space was used for storing supplies, ammunition, torpedoes, and living quarters for officers and crew. The size of the crew surprised me. Given the amount of storage required for patrols, the space available for sleeping quarters and supplies of food required for long cruises, a crew of 80 didn't leave a lot of open space anywhere on the boat.

Moving into the main body of the boat, we found it much larger than expected and the distribution and storage spaces were sufficient for a rather normal existence. Besides the captain, there were other officers onboard with responsibilities for the operation and maintenance of equipment and numerous instruments governing the control of the ship's operations. Submarine crews are highly skilled and able to operate a number of positions in addition to their primary assignment. With the exception of a small number of seamen, the remaining members of the crew were various levels of Petty Officers with years of experience. The importance of being able to perform a number of jobs efficiently was of great importance in the event a member of the crew were injured or incapacitated. There had to be people sufficiently trained to take over vital functions. Emergencies take place at sea, far from any Naval Station where crew members can be exchanged expeditiously. In most instances they are not able to surface and replace personnel especially with the qualifications required of submarine personnel.

Given the fact the boat was much larger inside than I had imagined, every inch of the ship was occupied. The passageways were narrow but not crowded. It did have the basics for living areas like bunks, kitchen, mess hall, etc. The bunks were attached to the bulkhead and located wherever space allowed, including over the torpedoes. "Officers' Country" had limited space but was efficiently furnished.

When we left the harbor to go out to sea, we sailed on the surface of the ocean where the sub rose and fell with the movement of the waves much as would be experienced in a destroyer or smaller ship at sea. The weather was normal for the Atlantic, having no severe wave action but enough movement to react like any other surface vessel. When we reached the area where we were to make our dives, the hatches were closed and locked.

The experience of going under the surface of the ocean was amazing. On the surface the sub rolled and reacted to the waves. As soon as we submerged, the ride became absolutely smooth, comfortable. We made a number of dives and gradually became accustomed to the changes we experienced on and under the surface of the ocean. I believe the closed atmosphere of the sub would have been a serious problem for someone suffering from claustrophobia. Apparently no one in our class had this problem. Given the huge size of submarines in operation today, using nuclear power allows the boat to stay submerged for months at a time without the need to surface for a transfer of fuel and supplies. This exercise left some of us wishing the subs had space available for a chaplain.

Following this experience, we returned to our base, completed our training program and received orders to our first duty stations. I was assigned to the 5th Marines, Pendleton, California, and could not be happier about this assignment. The program ended with a graduation ceremony where some of the wives were present. Several of us bought a fifth of vodka and poured it in the punch bowl on the main table. No one noticed the improved flavor of the drink or showed any signs of distaste. Later we discovered it wasn't such a novel idea as every previous graduating class did the same thing.

Chapter 3
Trip to Camp Pendleton

T wo of us received orders to the West Coast and made the trip together. We were given 11 days to pack up and move to our first assignments. A Jesuit priest in our group was assigned to a naval base in California, and I had an assignment to the Fifth Marines, stationed in Pendleton, California. A car I had for several years proved appropriate for this trip. I picked him up in Chicago. Being single, neither of us had much luggage to carry. All of it easily fit in the trunk of my car. We decided to travel the famous Route 66, steeped in American history. We were determined to make this trip an enjoyable experience taking advantage of the week we had to report to duty. This proved to be the right decision.

We made a decision to visit as many tourist attractions as time allowed. Although we stopped at a lot of them, some captured our attention more than others. The first stop in our journey was the Gateway Arch in St. Louis, Missouri.

The Gateway Arch

As we entered St. Louis, we discovered immediately it would not be difficult to find the Gateway Arch. The memorial is so huge it towers over everything around it. When we purchased our tickets, we picked up a few leaflets discussing the structure. Some facts are worth mentioning. This arch is the world's tallest arch, the tallest monument in the Western Hemisphere, and the tallest accessible building in Missouri. An impressive stainless steel structure 630 ft. high with rides to the top encouraged us to make the trip. The conveyance was a small tub-like vehicle with enough room to hold two people, in a somewhat compressed fashion. The ride was swift, ending in a long, narrow chamber with windows allowing us to have a great view of the city. About a dozen other visitors moved around the area, taking pictures and commenting on how well it represented the country's westward development. Our stopover at the Arch proved to be a great beginning; the first of several memorable sites we visited while driving Route 66 from Chicago to our duty stations on the West Coast.

As we traveled west and entered western Oklahoma, we encountered a major change in the topography that would characterize the landscape for most of the trip. Tall trees disappeared and were replaced with bushes. The land was flat, dry with mesa formations, each stretching for several miles. Living in mid-America with forest, hills, and abundant water sources, the atmosphere along Route 66 was dry and hot. It gave us feeling of being in a wide open space unencumbered by tall buildings, thick forests, and crowds of people hurrying to and from work. It was a relaxing atmosphere, making the travel a pleasant ride.

Meteor Crater

The next major attraction was the meteor crater in Arizona. The surface in the area was flat with very little vegetation. I do not remember seeing a tree anywhere. Arriving at the meteor, its size and depth were truly captivating. There was a platform at the top of the crater, exposing this massive hole in the ground. Scientists tell us the crater was caused by a 300,000 ton meteor 130 feet in diameter travelling at 22,000 mph when it hit the plateau. When the meteor crashed into the desert floor, it left a 2.4 mile wide, 550 ft. deep crater. All other forms of life nearby became extinct in seconds. This event took place around 50,000 years ago. One almost unbelievable fact is when it hit it blew 175 million tons of rock and dirt into the air! The force of the winds blew the debris everywhere. However, driving to and from the site, there appeared to be no surface signs indicating these changes were still around. Now, whenever I see a shooting star I am delighted to see it burn up when it hits our atmosphere.

Petrified Forest and Painted Desert

The Petrified Forest and the Painted Desert, although different, have a great deal in common. They lay alongside each other, and extraordinary forces formed both. The Petrified Forest had its beginnings over 225 million years ago. Over time, the trees were uprooted and covered with sediment, eventually turning the trees into quartz, a very hard material only able to be cut by diamond-tipped saws. The trees are scattered all over the area.

The information at the park station explained the course of nature's actions this way: "Water seeping through the wood replaced decaying organic material cell by cell with multicolored silica. Eventually, the land where the great logs were buried was lifted up by geological upheaval, and wind and rain began to wear away the overlying sediments, finally exposing the long-buried, now petrified wood."

Standing a few feet away from the trees, the trunks still looked like wood. But touching one and trying to move it told us this is no normal tree. The logs and the chips of petrified rock scattered around the ground were surprisingly hard and heavy. The trees turned to quartz weighed about 200 pounds per cubic foot. I don't recall picking up samples during our visit, but now I wished I had. They could be a reminder: God's work takes time, but the results are beautiful.

As we drove out of the Petrified Forest, we immediately entered the Painted Desert. Early evening had just set in and the sun was about ready to pack it in for the night. A light cloud cover and dark shadows were moving over the surface of the Painted Desert's rock formations, giving them a quiet, mysterious atmosphere. The changing colors and formation of the stones could keep a painter busy for a lifetime. The landscape looked like a painter's board with smears of lavender, white, yellow and red sediments stretching as far as the eye could see— absolutely beautiful.

Grand Canyon

We continued our drive to the Grand Canyon, arriving at the hotel in time for dinner and a good sleep. The hotel was located on the south rim of the canyon. We registered and selected rooms overlooking the canyon. After taking the bags to our rooms and freshening up a bit, we met for dinner in the hotel restaurant. I was ready for a good meal and a night's rest. Sitting next to our table was a young couple enjoying each other's company. Unknown to us, they had plans to take the same trip down the same side of the canyon wall to which we were assigned.

The next morning we met for breakfast, walked to the stables, and prepared for the ride down the south side canyon wall. There were a dozen or more huge mules grazing in a corral, waiting to take a tourist to the phantom ranch built alongside the Colorado River at the bottom of the canyon. The size of the mules was probably a necessary qualification to carry tourists down the canyon wall and then back up the trail to the corral. The complete trip was 19.5 miles long. We could have walked the trail, as others did, but the groups we saw walking back up the trail were taking frequent stops to regain their strength. Taking the mule ride made a lot of sense.

There were about eight people in our group waiting in the corral for the trail boss. When he arrived, he began by assigning each of us to a mule and checked each of our saddles to ensure they were properly strapped on the animal. At his signal, we started toward an opening in the rocky surface leading into the canyon. For me, the ride from the stables to the canyon opening was the most pleasant part of the whole trip. We entered the passageway, and as a path opened out into the canyon proper, we were amazed at the distance between the canyon walls. I looked down to the bottom of the canyon, a full mile straight down, and knew immediately this ride was probably a major mistake because my mule had an affection for walking on the outer edge of the trail. With my stirrups and knees I tried to encourage him to walk in the middle of the path, where both of us could make the trip in a safer manner. Walking at the edge of the path seemed much too close. I would try to move him toward the center of the path, but this dumb ass (if this term applies to mules as well as donkeys) would have no part of my suggestion. I tried to encourage it nicely, telling him how much safer it would be if he just moved a few feet closer to the center of the trail.

About a quarter of the way down, the mule saw some grass on the edge of the trail and decided to go after it. He turned, facing the open canyon, and bent his neck all the way down to the grass. He started eating it as I realized I was looking down his neck. To me it looked like the top of a slide with the bottom of the canyon as a destination! I pulled the reins back, understanding this was my signal to turn back to the middle of the trail and continue the trip in a safe way like the other mules were doing. Ticked off, I told him what I thought of his mental competence, at which he took no umbrage.

However, the trail boss apparently heard my discussion with his animal. He leaned back, looked at me, and said, "We have never lost a mule on this ride."

My response may not have been the most courteous, but I it came directly from my heart. "I don't give a damn about this mule. I don't like his eating habits or his affection for walking the edge of the trail." Later in life I learned about the "horse whisperer" approach to training horses to cooperate with the rider. It's probably a good thing I was unaware of the process, because what I would have whispered into his ear would have probably motived him to toss me over the side!

For the rest of the trip to the bottom, the mule walked on the edge of the path eating grass wherever he saw any. Actually, the mule walked wherever he wished, eating grass wherever he found it. The only thing he didn't do was give me the finger, only because he didn't have one. I would have volunteered to walk back but the tail boss needed someone to drive this beast back to the corral.

The newly married couple was a part of our group. The lady rode side saddle all the way down and back up the trail. She looked brave...until I realized she was facing the wall of the canyon and if the mule decided to take a shortcut to the bottom she could just slide off it and land safely onto the middle of the trail. When we returned to the corral, I got off the mule and felt like it should have been transported to a meat factory. It was large enough to feed a mink farm for several weeks.

At the evening dinner, we again sat at a table a few feet from where the young couple was sitting. They finished dinner sooner than we did. When they finished eating, her husband got up and went to assist her. Her legs were so stiff she had difficulty trying to stand up and an equally difficult time trying to walk to the door. Apparently she was stiff from the ride, which does not speak highly of riding a mule side saddle for any length of time—especially down the canyon wall. The next morning, we left Flagstaff and drove to Los Angles, passing through Barstow, California, where I would eventually spend two years as the Marine Battalion Catholic Chaplain.

Romanoff's Restaurant

We often heard movie celebrities frequented Romanoff's restaurant in LA. So we decided to have dinner there and see some of the movie stars. We took a table, had a cocktail, and placed an order. Looking around the room, we noticed there were about a dozen people in the dining room. We were waiting for the stars to enter, and I believe the other guests were doing the same thing. The service and food were excellent but no celebrity entered the place. After an hour or so we left, believing the rumor about the restaurant filled with movie stars must have come from the time of the silent movies when Romanoff's was big time in a small town. When the trip ended, we were happy we decided to drive Route 66. Over the years, I've driven Route 66 several times, but without ever stopping at Romanoff's again.

Chapter 4
Historical Origins of Chaplains in the Military

C haplains in the military should not come as a surprise if you will remember our country was founded by Europeans who came here to enjoy the freedom to practice their religions. America and the free practice of religion have always had a sacred relationship. Our Founding Fathers and other colonists lived and worked together without government interference in the manner in which they practiced their faiths. This respect for each citizen's right to live their faith was a powerful motivator for thousands of people who made an inconvenient and very dangerous trip to our shores. This and other acts of freedom allowed them to thrive and succeed in their own efforts, not subject to a relationship with royalty or the wealthy.

Having chaplains in the military has a history extending thousands of years into human history. This relationship between the worship of God and the military's practice of religion didn't start a few hundred years ago. Having priests petition God for their success in times of war and other important occasions was characteristic of both pagan nations and the Jews. Although they did not worship in the same manner, they did acknowledge the existence of God and paid homage to the Creator. A testament to this practice has been found wherever civilizations existed. A part of this discovery includes the identification of priests (chaplains) acting as emissaries between their fighting forces and God, seeking heaven's help as they engaged in the battle. This was especially true in times of great concern.

The Jewish nation and the Old Testament are the foundations of Christianity. Jewish priests (chaplains in their armed forces) were actively involved with the military, offering prayers for their success in the fields of battle as well as for divine assistance in other important issues of the day. This was especially visible in their struggle against the Canaanites.

Of the many battles in which the Jewish nation engaged, one which triggers our memories is found in Exodus 17:11. Israel was engaged in a very difficult war with the Amalekites in Rephidim. Moses, with his hands raised, prayed for the victory of the Israelites. As long as he held up his arms while praying, the Israelites would win the battle. But as his arms began to tire, he lowered them—at which time the Amalekites would start winning. Aaron and Hur sat Moses on a stone and held up his arms, resulting in a victory for the Israelites. This and other such events show God's close attention to and care for the Jewish people. This relationship was personal and emotional. It was an association of friends, as God's presence and constant assistance intermingled in all their life activities.

Chaplains Have Been A Part of the U.S. Military Since the Revolutionary War

The presence of chaplains in our Armed Forces has a history extending back to the Revolutionary War, when George Washington insisted chaplains be assigned to each regiment of the army and insisted officers and men attend Sunday morning services. This directive was extended to include naval personnel as well. His deep faith in the providence of God and his reliance on God's assistance to create a new, independent nation was rewarded even beyond his vision of America's future. This same faith in God was a major influence in the lives and activities of all the Founding Fathers. The citizens' right to worship God, to have religious services and speak freely about God and His teaching, was cemented into the foundation of this nation and clearly stated in the First Amendment to the Constitution:

> "Congress shall make no law respecting an establishment of religion, or prohibiting the free exercise thereof; or abridging the freedom of speech, or of the press; or the right of the people peaceably to assemble, and to petition the Government for a redress of grievances."

Today, thousands of chaplains continue to create appropriate opportunities for our military personnel and their families to bring God into their lives and allow His teachings to be the foundation for a principled life.

A Department of Defense policy continues to enforce the right of military personnel to practice their religion freely:

> "The U.S. Constitution proscribes Congress from enacting any law prohibiting the free exercise of religion. The Department of Defense places a high value on the rights of members of the Military Services to observe the tenets of their respective religions. DOD policy that requests for accommodation of religious practices should be approved by commanders when accommodation will not have an adverse impact on mission accomplishment, military readiness, unit cohesion, standards, or discipline."

Department of Defense (DOD) regulations confirms the constitutional right of military personnel to practice their faiths and commanders are obligated to ensure this right is fulfilled and protected.

General George Washington and the Continental Congress Made Chaplains an Integral Part of the Armed Forces

General George Washington, in command of the Continental Army in 1775, was a man of deep faith, fully aware of his dependence on God and the need for prayer in all aspects of his life. Believing military personnel had the same need for God's influence, he introduced the chaplaincy into the Continental Army, insisting they be treated and paid as officers in the army, and be obligated to offer Sunday religious services for his troops. To this end, he established the chaplaincy with this directive to the Continental Congress, on July 20, 1775:

> "The Hon. Continental Congress having been pleased to allow a Chaplain to each Regiment, with the pay of Thirty-three Dollars and one third per month – The Colonels or commanding officers of each regiment are directed to procure Chaplains accordingly; persons of good characters and exemplary lives–To see that all

inferior officers and soldiers pay them a suitable respect and attend carefully upon religious exercises. The blessing and protection of Heaven are at all times necessary but especially so in times of public distress and danger–The General hopes and trusts, that every officer and man, will endeavor so to live, and act, as becomes a Christian Soldier defending the dearest Rights and Liberties of his country."

Regardless of one's specific religious beliefs, Washington made certain all soldiers, officers and men, be given the opportunity to worship God. In the orders Washington gave at Middlebrook on 28 June 1777, he insisted on this position as follows:

"... all Chaplains are to perform divine services tomorrow and on every succeeding Sunday, with their respective brigades and regiments, where the situation will possibly admit of it. And the Commanding officers of the corps are to see that they attend themselves with officers of all ranks setting the example. The Commander in Chief expects an exact compliance with this order, and that it be observed in the future as an invariable rule and practice. And every neglect will be considered not only as a breach of orders, but a disregard to decency, virtue and religion."

For George Washington, the Continental Congress and the citizens of this great nation, the worship of Almighty God was not an optional matter. His position was always "Freedom of Religion" without any hint congress meant "freedom from religion." He insisted all officers and men attend religious services on Sundays, without restricting prayer to Sunday services only.

There are numerous examples of General Washington kneeling in prayer before entering into combat. Of all the remarkable events for which he is credited, his prayer life and the promotion of prayer among the troops would receive special recognition. It seems obvious God played a major part in the revolutionary war. What else could account for this "rag tag" army made up of farmers, shop keepers, fishermen, bakers, carpenters, tailors and printers defeating the greatest military power of the age? Everyday citizens went into combat with the most powerful, highly trained, and successful army in the world, won their freedom, and formed a new nation. They accomplished the impossible, with the help of God. Prayers for God's help were answered and a new country was born with a destiny to become the world's first government to be ruled by its citizens; a status won by citizens who were free, at peace and enjoyed the gift of liberty. Most importantly, they found a place for God at everyone's table and have been richly rewarded.

Dozens of religious creeds offering spiritual guidance to citizens flourish in our society. The direction of General Washington did not identify any specific religious faith be practiced. His direction insists whatever faith the soldier practiced, he would be allowed and directed to do so at Sunday services. This Constitutional directive has been continued since the foundation of our nation. Since then the Chaplains Corps has been an active unit of the armed forces in every branch of our military service.

Any study of the life of George Washington discovers he was a man of prayer. Of the dozens of examples of his dedication to prayer and to his faith life, I selected two incidents to confirm this fact in Washington's life.

The first story about Washington's prayer life concerns a 26 year old Quaker pacifist, Isaac Potts, whose home in Valley Forge was being used as the Continental Army's Commanding General Headquarters. He observed George Washington kneeling, deeply engrossed in prayer. He related this experience to Rev. Nathaniel Snowden.

The nearest to an authentication of the Potts story of Washington's prayer in the woods is supplied by the *Diary and Remembrances* of the Rev. Nathaniel Randolph Snowden, an ordained Presbyterian minister, graduate of Princeton with a degree from Dickinson College. The Historical Society of Pennsylvania owns the original. Mr. Snowden was born in Philadelphia January 17, 1770 and died November 12, 1851. His writings cover a period from his youth to 1846. In his records are found these observations, in Mr. Snowden's own handwriting:

"I knew personally the celebrated Quaker Potts who saw Gen'l Washington alone in the woods at prayer. I got it from himself, myself. Weems mentioned it in his history of Washington, but I got it from the man myself, as follows:

'I was riding with him (Mr. Potts) in Montgomery County, Penn' near to the Valley Forge, where the army lay during the war of yé Revolution. Mr. Potts was a Senator in our State and a Whig. I told him I was agreeably surprised to find him a friend to his country as the Quakers were mostly Tories. He said, "It was so and I was a rank Tory once, for I never believed that America did proceed against Great Britain whose fleets and armies covered the land and ocean, but something very extraordinary converted me to the Good Faith!" "What was that," I inquired? "Do you see those woods, and that plain? It was about a quarter of a mile off from the place we were riding, as it happened." "There," said he, "laid the army of Washington. It was a most distressing time of yé war, and all were for giving up the Ship but that great and good man. In that woods pointing to a close in view, I heard a plaintive sound as of a man at prayer. I tied my horse to a sapling and went quietly into the woods and to my astonishment I saw the great George Washington on his knees alone, with his sword on one side and his cocked hat on the other. He was at Prayer to the God of the Armies, beseeching to interpose with his Divine aid, as it was yé Crisis, the cause of the country, of humanity and of the world."

"Such a prayer I never heard from the lips of man. I left him alone praying.'"

On Saturday, May 2, 1778, General George Washington issued the following orders to his troops from his Headquarters at Valley Forge:

"General Orders

Head-Quarters V. Forge Saturday May 2nd 78.

The Commander in Chief directs that divine Service be performed every Sunday at 11 o'clock in those Brigades to which there are Chaplains—those which have none to attend the places of worship nearest to them—It is expected that Officers of all Ranks will by their attendance set an Example to their men.

While we are zealously performing the duties of good Citizens and soldiers we certainly ought not to be inattentive to the higher duties of Religion—To the distinguished Character of Patriot, it should be our highest Glory to add the more distinguished Character of Christian—The single instances of providential Goodness which we have experienced and which have now almost crowned our labors with complete success, demand from us in a peculiar manner the warmest returns of Gratitude & Piety to the Supreme Author of all Good. ...

The Commander in Chief approves the sentence and orders it to take place.

After Orders May 2nd 1778

No fatigue Parties to be employed on Sundays till further Orders.

This directive clearly states the position of George Washington. He believed the success of the military rested in God's providence, and he insisted military personnel acknowledge and appreciate the help and protection they have received in their struggle to be free of English rule and establish a nation giving everyone freedom and liberty. His position on God and man's need to acknowledge God's place in our lives, is clearly stated in this phrase "it is the duty of all nations to acknowledge the providence of Almighty God, to obey His will, to be grateful for His benefits, and humbly to implore His protection and favor."

When Washington encountered practices belittling the religious beliefs of other personnel, he refused personally to engage in them and on one occasion objected to his command participating in them. This was made clear when he was invited to attend "Guy Fawkes Night" during which anti-Catholic sentiment was expressed by burning an effigy of the pope. His belief that citizens had a right to practice without ridicule was an absolute. This program was never held again.

Since the Revolution

Following the Revolutionary War, military operations have experienced countless changes in their manner of operation, the equipment used for combat and the extent of our involvement throughout the world. The presence of chaplains in all the Armed Forces is an operation that has not changed. The needs of our military now, spiritually, are the same as they were when General Washington commanded the Colonial Army. In Washington's time, as is presently the case, chaplains are a part of the military, hold an officer's rank, and live with the troops. His great respect for God and his private and public display of faith were hallmarks of his manner of leadership. At a Thanksgiving proclamation, he describes our nation's relationship with God as follows:

"The people of these States" devote themselves in service to "that great and glorious Being who is the beneficent author of all the good that was, that is, or that will be." It urges the people in the young country to express their gratitude to God for His protection of them through the Revolutionary War and the peace they had experienced since, for allowing the Constitution to be composed in a "peaceable and rational manner;" for the "civil and religious liberty" they possessed; and "in general, for all the great and various favors which He has been pleased to confer upon us." The proclamation also states "it is the duty of all nations to acknowledge the providence of Almighty God, to obey His will, to be grateful for His benefits, and humbly to implore His protection and favor." (Washington Thanksgiving Proclamation, Oct. 3, 1789).

In 1790, his dedication ensuring freedom of religion for everyone was clearly expressed in a letter he wrote to the Hebrew Congregation in Newport. Rhode Island. His letter stated, "May the Children of the Stock of Abraham, who dwell in this land, continue to merit and enjoy the good will of the other Inhabitants; while everyone shall sit in safety under his own vine and fig tree, and there shall be none to make him afraid."

A must read is President Washington's final address to Congress. The address concentrates on principles basic to an effective management of government. His understanding of human nature and the impact it has on decision making in matters of governance demonstrated an extraordinary grasp of the relationship between the law and the lawmakers. His advice on what our nation's relationships should be with foreign governments should be a primer for all those newly elected to Congress as well as those who have made elected office a career. He insisted the Almighty be acknowledged and worshiped giving the success of our nation as a proof that God answers prayers. The presence of Chaplains and the support of religious practices in the Armed Forces demonstrate Washington's advice on religious practice in the military and are practiced in our Armed Forces today.

Chapter 5

Average Age of Military Personnel
is 19 Years Young

T here are several important elements characteristic of military personnel:

The officer corps makes up about 16% of the Armed Forces, enlisted around 84%.

The average age of our troops is 19 years old. This tells us they are just out of high school, probably lived with parents and siblings, and, for the most part, were supported by their parents.

They lived under the guidance of their parents until they entered the Armed Forces. They worship God in the manner their families practiced their faith.

Given the needs of the Service, their growth to maturity will take place rapidly. Up to that point, they have had very little if any really serious responsibilities in their lives. Understanding this is not true of all 19 year olds, it certainly describes the experience of most young men and women of that age. Entering the service is the first opportunity they have had to be totally responsible for managing their own lives, controlling their personal behavior, and for accepting and carrying out responsibilities involving their lives and those serving with them. A lesson they learn from the first day they enter the military is they are part of a disciplined unit, where everyone, including them, needs each other to succeed and survive.

Education & Work History

Upon enlistment in the Armed Forces, the recruit finds himself in a position of making moral judgments based on principles that will guide his life. His course of action will be determined by the application of moral values drawn from the code of morality developed in his environment at home and the impact of his associates and society. From here on, his moral code will be in his hands, refined by the performance of his job and the direction and example set by supervisors and his associations and religious leaders.

The demands made on them immediately calls for maturity in the way they respond to all facets of military life. They meet life head-on, alone, although surrounded by hundreds of personnel all of whom are adjusting to pressures and difficulties that make up their everyday experiences. Unlike the freedom they experienced at home and in school, what they do now and how they do it are highly regulated and under constant surveillance. As their competence level develops, close supervision diminishes and their responsibilities increase.

Education and training play a major role throughout their tour. The knowledge and skills necessary to operate weapons systems with unimaginable, destructive force does not allow for careless or misinformed procedures. The training they receive is designed to ensure they are mentally and physically prepared to operate whatever weapons fall to their charge. For example, there must be certainty those authorized to operate highly technical equipment are fully knowledgeable of the systems involved and of the amount of destructive power the weapon is capable of inflecting.

To arrive at that competence level, several levels of training are required. The recruit goes through basic training, a period of intense physical and psychological training, absorbing every hour of their day. Night time finds them totally exhausted hoping to awake the next morning capable of meeting the next day's demands. By the end of boot camp, the 98 pound weakling is a fully developed Marine or sailor ready to carry his weight wherever called for.

I recall a graduate from Catholic Central, Marquette, who enlisted in the Marines following graduation. He wasn't exactly a 98 pound weakling, but neither was he an example of physical prowess. I will never forget seeing him walking down Front Street in Marquette, in his Marine uniform demonstrating an attitude of confidence and strength that seemed to say "I'm a Marine. I can take on the whole world."

After basic training, the troops are advanced to training programs in the specialties which they have chosen or to which they have been assigned. They will become immersed in technology and equipment ultimately becoming one of their primary assignments. As technology and equipment advance there is a need for constant updating by those responsible for the maintenance and operation of newly developed weaponry. Our rapid advance in the sciences results in training being a never-ending process.

A benefit that has allowed many professionals to earn a degree is the military program of paying for a student's college education. College education has become so expensive that many very competent people are unable to meet the costs involved. Allowing the military to assist in meeting college costs is an extraordinary advantage. The price is a few years in the Service as an officer with the right to remain in the Service or complete the required years and return to a civilian career.

Several years ago, two young men entered college with a goal of become medical doctors. After several years of meeting education expenses, it became an impossible goal even with financial help from their parents. To take a loan would have put them in debt for years. A suggestion was made that they enlist in the Navy as medical students and allow the Service to take care of their medical education expenses. At first, there was great reluctance to take that step, but eventually both took the advice and joined the Navy. The result was amazing. All their college costs were taken care of. They were commissioned as officers, and while they were completing their medical education, they received a salary that paid their living expenses throughout their years in medical school. During vacation periods, they were assigned to various military hospitals, putting their training into practice. Upon receiving their doctorates, they were advanced in grade and were assigned to duty at Navy hospitals. One of them completed his obligated time in the service and returned to civilian life and practice, while the other remained in the Navy as his career field. Neither of them would have completed their medical education without the assistance of the Navy. Both parties, as well as the Navy, benefited immensely because of this program.

Military Life Is Physically And Mentally Demanding

Life in the military is demanding physically and mentally. Watching the SEALs' naval training program on television leaves all of us amazed at the demands made of these men. Physically, they are trained to endure exhaustion, hunger, thirst, freezing cold temperatures, and extreme heat. They learn to control fear, swim 350 feet under water, and hold their breath under water for two minutes. The broad scope of their training for combat and the expertise they acquire in the use of weapons allows them to operate successfully any place in the world. In a sense, they become weapons themselves. Although the Army Delta Force would disagree on this point, the SEALs are the best combat unit anywhere in the world. This service seldom looks for volunteers. The Navy researches its personnel and selects those it believes could succeed as a Navy SEAL. Recent events in the Middle East brought to light the exceptional competence of the Navy SEALs. It is reassuring to know we have so competent and dedicated a unit covering our backs, ensuring the safety of our nation.

There are thousands of positions that do not call for extreme physical competence, like technicians sitting at their desks in Virginia controlling a drone flying over a building in Iraq. They may be ready to put a missile down the chimney of a house shortly after the target arrives or takeout one specific car among several travelling rapidly in a caravan. Pilots flying aircraft travelling at the speed of sound equipped with Phoenix missiles that can hit a target 100 miles away, armed infrared sensors that can lay a bomb on a target with absolute accuracy. Aircraft carriers, destroyers, and submarines are unmatched for the quality of craftsmanship and unreal competence required to carry out their missions anywhere in the world. Accepting the almost unimaginable competencies found in our military world, the entire operation rests on the management and operational skills of the men and women in our Armed Force.

The control and use of our weapons and sophisticated military equipment rests in the hands of Marines, sailors and soldiers who were born and raised on the countless farms, towns, and cities throughout the US; attended our schools, and grew up neighbors living next door. Today, these are the men and women defending our nation. From boot camp until they leave the Service, their duties will call for every bit of energy they can muster; performance that initially exceeds their known competence level and exposure to harm, serious injury, perhaps death, and having the strength to control fear while every bone in their body tells them to run for cover. Although always aware of their personal worth and competence there is a basic understanding their value is measured by participation as a member of their unit whose combined action can accomplish otherwise impossible tasks.

Influence of Background and Personality

When entering the service, one of the first lessons learned is responsibility for their personal lives. An honest review of life before that event reveals many people did not actually have responsibility for major portions of their lives. Mom and dad generally furnished housing, food, transportation, entertainment, clothing, school expenses, taking care of all things necessary for their survival. School administrators, teachers, coaches, and maintenance staff ensured a learning environment and direction to intellectual growth. The pastor and parishioners brought God into their lives, affording them the opportunity to learn and live their faiths. All of these interacted with them, generally with gentle concern for their feelings, making serious efforts to guide while doing so in a respectful manner.

Immediately upon being sworn into the military, nearly all these disappear. The world they have now entered accepts the recruit as an adult fully aware of the need for physical strength, mental awareness, and a deep respect for authority that will direct their lives for the length of their tour.

However, although living in a world that demands strict obedience in many areas of their lives, they now experience a new liberty, a freedom to manage their lives responsibly, making strides toward an adult maturity. This will be the experience of nearly all recruits. A few will fall short of these standards and experience penalties designed to correct and avoid unacceptable behavior.

Military Training – A Route To Maturity

Training and most other assignments demanded of the Naval/Marine services require dedication and competence in all areas of military life. Their training programs do not involve all the extremities found in the training and life of a Navy SEAL but do require a total commitment to the physical and mental demands made on them. Training is intense and continuous. Knowledge of their equipment and its use is vital to their survival and the successful accomplishment of their missions. Given the average age of our military personnel, 19 years old, it is amazing to realize the extraordinary responsibilities committed to their care and their willingness to accept this trust, fully aware of the responsibilities involved. We know men and women of the Armed Forces are some of best people of our nation. The experience they have serving in the Armed Forces gives them a respect for authority, an understanding of people's strengths and weaknesses, and the need for discipline to accomplish a project successfully. We should evaluate entrance into the military as a training system for future national leaders. Being accustomed to placing the welfare of our nation over their personal safety gives them the capacity to work for the best interests of the country, even when political expediency would advise otherwise.

Military Life is an Extension of Civilian Life

It is important to remember that the military is an extension of society in general. Customs, attitudes, morals, and other principles governing the lives of the citizens in our society carry over into the lives of our military personnel. As we enter the 21st century, major philosophical changes are sweeping across the most important elements of our lives. The supremacy of state governments seems to be squished under the mountain of federal regulations pressing down their prerogative to govern themselves. The sense of law and order was the hallmark of our society. In many ways it appears to be inoperative, as our permissive society finds crime excusable because of difficult social concerns. An insightful article written October 31, 2014 by

David H. Folz and Cameron Dodd was quoted in the ASPA publication on June 1, 2015.

What on earth is going on here? Can the litany of government scandals that seem to erupt <u>weekly have anything to do with the lack of training in the foundational values and principles</u> of the republic?

Just a few of the things that are not supposed to occur in a government administered by competent, ethically aware and professionally trained leaders sensitive to the first principles of a constitutional system include:

- *Veterans Affairs hospitals that delay or deny health care to thousands of combat veterans.*

- *Internal Revenue Service targeting conservatives and other groups and then "losing" relevant records that may incriminate government officials.*

- *Executive orders that exempt or defer selected groups from various provisions of federal health care laws.*

- *Selective enforcement and non-enforcement of federal immigration laws.*

- *Bureau of Alcohol, Tobacco, Firearms and Explosives scheme that allows illegal straw buyers to acquire thousands of firearms, some of which are linked to later killings of Mexican civilians and a U.S. border patrol agent.*

- *Centers for Disease Control and Prevention loss of credibility with every news conference about Ebola.*

There is abundant evidence of an abysmally low level of understanding of the constitution, our system of government, and American history in general."

Public schools prohibit the use of God's name in school functions or use of prayer before, during, or after a sporting event. Classes on American History present the USA as a rogue nation, concealing the facts that made this the greatest nation in the history of the world. No mention is made of the actions we made to rebuild Europe and Japan, former enemies, after the second World War; the Berlin Airlift that saved the lives of millions of Berliners as Communist Russia attempted to starve the citizens to death; building the Panama Canal, which revolutionized shipping lanes, benefiting commerce worldwide; construction of a network of US highways, making easy access between the states, expanding commerce nationwide and helping to pull together the oneness of our nation. It appears that our school systems have either neglected to teach civic courses or do not give it the attention this study deserves to enable our citizens to be knowledgeable of the principles that allow citizens ultimately to control government. The price for this neglect could be the loss of or freedoms/liberty.

Chapter 6

Chaplain's Life Work is Bringing God
to the Troops and the Troops to God

This is accomplished by conducting formal religious services, training programs, and administering the sacraments. Religious beliefs and the practice of our faiths remain the same, whether we are living in a military or civilian community. Our recognition of God and our obligation to acknowledge Him through prayer follows us throughout all phases of our lives. So entering the military carries with it the obligation to bring God and our relationship with Him into a new venue of our lives. Fortunately, for hundreds of years the military has been supportive of making opportunities available for military personnel to practice their religions.

Religious Life in the Military

Religious life in a military community has characteristics in most ways identical to those living in a civilian parish. Ceremonies involving baptism, weddings, and occasional funeral services are managed efficiently using the base chapel for the services. Conveniences like a room for the bride to do last minute preparations and sufficient space for guests to attend a wedding or funeral comfortably are available in the Base chapel. Its size, pews, and bathrooms make it a convenient location for Sunday Schools, Confirmation classes, baptismal and graduation ceremonies and other functions.

Aware of this, every Navy and Marine Base has a chapel, open 24 hours a day, where troops can enter and spend some quiet time with their Maker asking for direction in their lives and the ability to understand and resolve issues troubling them. The chaplains' offices are located in the same building, making it convenient to seek their assistance or discuss issues impacting their daily lives.

Living aboard a ship, this option generally is not available. An exception would be The USS *Shangri-La* (CVA 38). A chapel was installed while we were under repair at the Naval Ship Yard in Philadelphia, Pennsylvania. Fortunately, it was located mid-ship with easy access for both officers and enlisted men. It proved to be most convenient for daily Mass, confessions, and religious instructions.

Performing religious services with the Marines differed depending on the troop location. Stateside, a Marine Base would have a chapel where services would be held and have functions similar to those in a civilian parish. During field exercises, the convenience of a chapel is not available. So other arrangements are made for administering religious services in locations accessible to the troops. Generally, as witnessed in many movies, the hood of the jeep becomes the altar and the troops gather around it to participate in the service.

Counseling

Counseling, an important activity, absorbs a considerable amount of a chaplain's time. Many troops, especially new recruits, are away from home and friends for the first time in their lives. Although reluctant to admit it, they are lonesome. Eventually, they will make new and lasting friendships, but it takes time for close associations to develop. For some, taking orders leaving no room for questions is a bitter pill. But as their experience develops, the necessity of following orders is found to be indispensable.

Stationed stateside, chaplains participate in the base activities, which include counseling when personal problems or tragedy darkens their world. This is particularly important for the very young, inexperienced sailor or Marine who finds himself in unfamiliar circumstances, beyond his knowledge base to manage the situation. At times, the help they need is a sounding board—talking to someone in an open, confidential manner. Generally, the help they need is not assistance to come out of a deep depression; rather, they need help understanding a situation they had not previously encountered and to develop a plan of action to manage the issue appropriately. Characteristically, the chaplain will maintain confidentiality about the matter, ensuring no one will become privy to the conversation or issue. This confidentiality allows for an open, honest discussion of a problem, especially those involving marriages.

Omitting facts pertinent to the discussion can conceal the real issues needed for an accurate evaluation of the matter. Frequently, the subject omitted is the cause of the problem—e.g. I blew the money on the horses; I started using drugs and I don't know how to stop; I've been seeing this gal at work and she wants me to... and so forth. Getting to honesty is often the most difficult consideration to reach. Such problems have to be understood and dealt with to have any possibility of a reasonable resolution.

Other experiences take the wind out of their sails. Tragedies happen in both civilian and military lives. They are always painful and most often unexpected, like a car accident or heart attack. Less final but equally disturbing include divorce, addiction to illegal drugs, teen pregnancy and children with disabilities as well as those who are having difficulties in school activities, or are involved in a serious violation of civilian or military law.

Some family problems are caused by a lack of an appropriate opportunity to discuss disagreements reasonably. Their absence from the family unit makes this nearly impossible. Letters fail to clarify misunderstandings, resulting in hurt feelings and anger. In matters like this, the chaplain can be of assistance through marriage and personal counseling. At times working with chaplains at the home Base can be of assistance by communicating with the family stateside to resolve misunderstandings and hurt feelings. Experiencing difficult family issues does not happen just to younger personnel. Working on the premise couples do love one another, eventually workable solutions are developed and appreciated. The work of the chaplain, often unseen, becomes the catalyst that identifies the problem, develops the resolution, allowing the parties to normalize their communications.

Care for the Sick and Dying

Given the nature of the military activities, it is reasonable to understand accidents happen; people are hurt and hospitalized or family members become ill, needing immediate medical assistance. Perhaps more than most other occurrences, the chaplain must make time to visit them, see if they can be of assistance, and offer a prayer for their recovery. Even though the hospital has dozens of doctors, nurses, and other employees, it can be a lonely place. A visit by anyone, especially the chaplain and family members, helps to bring a little brightness to a boring, stressful, often painful time. The value of the chaplain's presence, asking for God's intervention or praying with the Marine, sailor, or family member as they prepare to leave this life is invaluable. For most of us, dying means leaving this life and entering the presence of God. To be by their side at this crucial time, praying and making the sacraments available to them, helps ease the transition into the presence of the Almighty. When family and friends are there, it is always strengthening to have the chaplain present to lead them in prayer and ask God to give them the strength to accept the loss they will continue to experience for some time into the future.

Recently, a close friend of mine passed away. For several months he remained at home, for the most part bedridden and very weak. I made it a point to visit him frequently to discuss the golf we played or the programs comprising a major part of the work we shared. Over the months, he kept telling me, "When I die, I want you here with me." I promised I would be there. Several months ago, I dropped by his home for a visit, and his wife told me he would not live out the day. I went to his bedside, sat down next to him, and told him I was present and would like to pray with him. Although he was not a Catholic, I whispered the Our Father prayer into his ear and after an act of sorrow for sins he committed I gave him absolution. I realize this was not a liturgically correct procedure, but he was a baptized Christian who did frequent church services and led an exemplary life. I wanted to do whatever I could to ensure he met God with a clear conscious. Someday, I plan on meeting him again in God's presence where he will say, "Thanks, Ray, for helping me get here safely."

Participating in Daily Life

Military Chaplains Live in Two Different Worlds:

First: The spiritual world: like the priest in civilian life, he fulfills his responsibilities by bringing faith to the troops through the sacraments, sermons, instructions, and other faith related programs.

Second: He becomes totally and personally a part of the military world, sharing their lives, work, successes, and failures.

The reduction in the size of our military personnel and the equipment needed to train and carry out their missions lessens their ability to train the military to function at the most effective and competent levels of engagement. Presently, we are under attack by Islamic extremists with a goal of destroying Israel and the USA and other Muslims with a different interpretation of the Koran and some Mid-East countries. It would be comforting to know our military is managing the problem with the support of the President and Congress. Our military has the awesome responsibility of protecting our county and requires total cooperation in meeting their needs to accomplish this task.

I spent four years with the Marines, serving stateside and in the Far East, and another four years serving with Naval Air on the aircraft carrier USS *Shangri-La* (CVA 38) in the Mediterranean and at the Ellyson Field Naval Air Station in Pensacola, Florida. My activities during this period are discussed later in this work. Serving in the military and participating in all the activities in which I was allowed to participate; long marches, field exercises, firing weapons, field training programs, throwing grenades, embarking and disembarking from troop ships, military exercises involving the use of helicopters and dozens of other activities composed the life of a Marine on active duty. In a lot of ways, my participation did not come close to that experienced by the troops. I was always comfortable being with them, sharing life in the world that was the Marines. The saying, "once a Marine, always a Marine" rang true for me. To this day, I cherish the friendships I have with the sailors and Marines I served with and their families, of whom I became a part.

Serving aboard an aircraft carrier and a naval air station, relationship with the personnel was the same but the location was very different. The work performed, and the energy required, was both physically exhausting and mentally demanding. Ship operation continued 24 hours a day, seven days a week. Flight operations took place during the day and at night, demanding the flight crew's constant attention to get their jobs done while avoiding the many hazards found on the flight desk. Receiving incoming aircraft while catapulting others while at the same time refueling aircraft and loading ammo does not allow for mistakes. Moving into a wrong area during flight operations could and has caused serious injury and death. Diesel fuel powered the USS *Shangri-La*. The heat generated by the ship's engines was so hot the crew working in the engine rooms had to move at a very slow pace to avoid being overcome by the heat. Noise was a permanent factor aboard ship, as work on the planes and the ship was an endless process.

Serving ashore at the Ellyson Naval Air Station was closely aligned to parish activities with Sunday and weekday masses, confessions, baptisms, instructions, weddings, and participation in base activities. Another major difference was the presence of other Catholic naval chaplains serving at stations located in and near Pensacola, Florida. The Eglin Air Force base, located a short drive from Pensacola, had several Catholic chaplains with whom we met on several occasions. About once a week, we would meet to play golf at the course on the Main Side Naval Air Station. While stationed in Pensacola, the PGA had a tournament, and each base was allowed to have one representative. At Ellyson we placed our names in a hat and someone drew the name of the winner. My name was drawn. I played the game, and some of the folks from the base followed me around to the very end. My score did not represent the base well, but my parents were visiting me at the time and they thought I did a marvelous job.

Some of these problems take time to uncover, and their sources are wrapped up in family matters long hidden from sight. Personal problems are often not clearly defined. Seeking the help of a chaplain and discussing the matter helps to clarify issues that lie at the root of the problem. At times the problem has its origin at home, where the wife must handle family matters by herself, often without input from the husband. Some problems may seem to be overwhelming as the husband is not present to discuss the issues and are too personal to discuss with neighbors or friends, such as managing family finances, disciplinary matters with the children, and some illnesses. At times an unresolved problem has damaging effects on the lives of all concerned.

Sometimes sailors at sea for a year's tour or a Marine stationed in the Far East for the second or third stint will receive a letter asking for a divorce because she is tired of handling family matters by herself without his assistance. She wants to relieve the pressure from all the activities overloading her life at home. A letter may arrive from his girlfriend notifying him she found someone else and her ring is in the mail, ending their relationship. This can happen without any indications it was waiting to happen. With reference to the girlfriend, this situation could be a gift from God since it could have happened after a marriage and children are caught in the middle of the struggle.

Chaplain's Duty to Persons of a Faith Other Than His

The primary attention of the chaplain is to work with members of his own faith ensuring their needs are met and their faith is kept alive while serving in the Armed Forces. As mentioned above, the Catholic chaplain makes the Mass and other Sacraments available to Catholics ensuring them access to his services with as little inconvenience as possible. This service often includes pre-marital and baptismal instructions and class instructions on the faith for those seeking to learn about the Catholic Church.

However, an important part of the chaplain's duties is ensuring all personnel wearing the uniform and their families have the opportunity to practice their faith; a right given them by the Constitution. This is especially important on bases or ship duty where there is only one chaplain assigned to the post. At times this involvement may call for the use of a civilian priest or minister to hold religious services on Sunday mornings where no naval chaplain is stationed. Additionally, the chaplain will assist Non-Catholics and those who do not subscribe to a specific faith with assistance in managing spiritual, personal and family problems.

Ultimately, the base commander or ship's captain can affect religious services by ensuring the command supports religious programs. This requires having time and space are made available for worship services. During my time in the Service, I was fortunate to have commanding officers who encouraged participation in religious services and sought their opinion on issues affecting the crew's well-being. My experience was full cooperation of the command, ensuring the practice of religion was encouraged and time and space made available to accommodate religious events.

Does God Have a Place in Today's Society?

The military experience, like the experience of civilian parishes, 18 to 25 year olds are not flocking to church services on Sundays morning. Why this is happening is not clear. Our relationship with the Creator and our total dependence upon Him should encourage everyone to acknowledge His existence in some fitting manner. The form this takes may differ from one faith practice to another, but the acknowledgement of God and our reliance on Him remains the same for everyone. Answering why this age group often fails to participate in worship services is not easy.

For those without a family background of attending church services and those where church and prayer were not a part of their lives, it is understandable why they do not attend services. But for those who attended Catholic school or other denominational school systems, this lack of attention to their religious life proves puzzling. What influence is so strong they reject the external practice of their religion and replace it with recreation or other activity?

Although not a complete answer, today's societal atmosphere carries much of the weight reflected in this decision process. Government is replacing God as the reliable source of help. Our welfare system, moral decay, divorces constantly out numbering marriages, and babies being killed in the womb by the millions might demonstrate our value systems are failing, and the results of this disaster is manifested in the lives of both military and civilian personnel. This whole movement is so contrary to the ideal of our founding fathers that even our Constitution is placed under fire from politicians who find it too restrictive for their permissive agendas.

Atheists, who hold God does not exist but believe we came from nothing, though minuscule in numbers, are managing to take God out of schools and public places against the will of an entire nation. The remark of a twelve year old public school child said volumes: "In our school God is illegal". In a society so infected, it is understandable why we have a lack of enthusiasm for an active practice of our religious beliefs.

Perhaps a part of the problem is a rebellion against years of family control and respect for religion no longer ushers them to Mass or other religious services. Our society, especially our public school system, finds no place for God in any of their activities, making it appear paying attention to God is a fairytale. It has no urgency, much less demand, to put time aside for the worship of God. Then on the other side of religious practice, we have radical Islam slaughtering hundreds of thousands of Christians and Jews and even other Muslims because they will not accept their version of religious beliefs, thus painting religion as a monstrous, cruel method for worshiping God.

Given the free run of drugs in our society, civilian pastors and military chaplains witness the destruction taking place in whole sections of our society. Although drugs have a detrimental impact on people of all ages, the most severely affected are the young, as their lives are gradually absorbed in satisfying their craving for satisfaction. School is no longer a safe haven, as it has become, in so many instances, a source of illegal drug distribution. Tens of thousands drop out of school as attendance hinders their greater access to drugs. The abuse of drugs creates a kind of rot that grows with the encouragement of state governments taxing the use of addiction as a source of increased income. Unbelievable!

Change in attitude toward a personal relationship with God requires more than the efforts of a chaplain, military or civilian. But wherever possible it is the chaplain who fights to keep God and His values foremost in the lives of military personal and their families.

Given the nature of man, having a body and soul, the demands of the body make the loudest noise and therefore receive the most attention. This condition can often drown out the soul's cry for recognition. Our inner life, our association with God expressed through prayer, and recognizing that our value as a person demands attention to spiritual values, becomes the mission of the chaplain.

The difficulty in carrying out this objective is society's concentration on evaluating man more as an animal than a person with both body and soul. Although this premise is understandable, it is necessary to recognize the unacceptable ramifications that follow this value system. The government becomes the sole lawmaker, functioning without regard to God and the attention He deserves from mankind. States bypass federal law and allow the use of illegal drugs as a source of tax income, fully aware of the human destruction drugs are causing throughout our societies. God is taken out of our school system, lest it offend an atheist who has no idea of the origin of our universe or can sensibly explain the order and complexities that so obviously govern our planet and universe.

In a recent visit to a doctor's office, I was examining a descriptive chart outlining the parts of a functioning ear. Its complexities were amazing. I was studying the chart when the doctor entered the room. "What a great proof of the existence of God. No way could this have developed by chance with the result of chance being a 50/50 possibility of success." He agreed and added the structure and functions of the eye are equally or even more proof all this came about by an intellect with infinite competence, which we know as God. This thinking, this acceptance of God and the place He has in our lives, has formed the principles on which this nation was founded and continues to affect the manner of our governance. In the military, the chaplain attempts to keep these principles alive and effective in the lives of our personnel.

All the important qualities required of a soldier, sailor, or Marine rests on spiritual values like love, respect, loyalty, sacrifice, mental competence, etc. It is in this arena where the work of the chaplain is found helping our military personnel and their families develop their entire persons, both body and soul.

George Washington insisted military personnel be afforded an opportunity to practice their faith. His life and that of the other Founding Fathers clearly show they considered this right to be a **freedom of religion, not freedom from religion.** His insistence that military personnel be given the opportunity to worship and that time is set aside every Sunday for religious services firmly establishes his intention that all his men should have the opportunity to practice their faith. His orders also include a command that soldiers be marched to services, clean and decent, and that officers must also attend the worship service. He wanted them to set a proper example of their recognition of God's favors and petition God for His assistance. There are dozens of paintings depicting the general on his knees acknowledging his dependence on God's favor. Probably the most recognized example has him kneeling in prayer with his horse standing next to him before the Battle of Valley Forge.

Chapter 7
Christians Can Have Powerful Enemies

It is a historical fact that Christians have forces opposed to their doctrine and moral code. That aggression began when Christ entered the scene 2000 years ago and has continued ever since. The Romans and other ancient civilizations resented their refusal to worship the many gods presented in the form of stone or metal images. Jews and Christians found them unacceptable, stating: "They have mouths, but they do not speak; they have eyes, but they do not see; They have ears, but they do not hear, nor is there any breath at all in their mouths…" These observations were not acceptable, resulting in severe punishment and deaths for countless Christians.

Many of us today are left in a quandary over the wholesale slaughter of Christians by the ISIS thugs rampaging throughout the Middle East, committing the most heinous killings experienced in our lifetime. Whether the US should step in and rid the world of their atrocities is basically the same problem that confronted Christianity in the Middle Ages when it became necessary to send the Crusaders to Jerusalem to stop the Muslims from slaughtering Christians and destroying their churches and other property. The crusades ended in 1291 on the coast of present day Israel.

In the very early years of our nation, the US experienced the barbarism of militant Islamism states resulting in our fighting two wars against them.

"The First Barbary War (1801–1805) also known as the Tripolitan War or the Barbary Coast War, was the first of two wars fought between the United States and the Northwest African Berber Muslim states known collectively as the Barbary States. These were the Ottoman provinces of Tripoli, Algiers, and Tunis, which enjoying a large autonomy, as well as the independent Sultanate of Morocco. The war was fought because U.S. President Thomas Jefferson refused to pay the high tributes demanded by the Barbary

States and because they were seizing American merchant ships and enslaving the crews for high ransoms. It was the first declared war the United States fought on foreign land and seas."

Obama can learn a lot about how we should be dealing with Islamic extremists from Thomas Jefferson.

From Downtrend:

In 1786, Jefferson and John Adams met with Tripoli's ambassador to Great Britain. They asked this 'diplomat' by what right his nation attacked American ships and enslaved her citizens and why the Muslims held such hostility toward this new nation, with which neither Tripoli nor any of the other Barbary Coast nations had any previous contact. The answer was as follows:

'[This nation] was founded on the Laws of their Prophet, that it was written in their Qur'an, that all nations who should not have acknowledged their authority were sinners, that it was their right and duty to make war upon them wherever they could be found, and to make slaves of all they could take as Prisoners, and that every Musselman [Muslim] who should be slain in battle was sure to go to Paradise.'

That is indeed quite revealing. Yet, America continued paying ransoms to these terrorists for the next fifteen years or so until Jefferson became President. Then, the Pasha (leader) of Tripoli sent a demand to the new leader for an immediate payment of $225,000 and $25,000 per year on an ongoing basis. Jefferson flatly refused, leading the Pasha to cut down the flagpole of the American consulate and declaring war on the United States. The rest of the terrorist states followed suit.

Jefferson had formerly been against raising a navy, but this soon changed as he was determined to meet force with force. A squadron of vessels was sent to the area, and Congress authorized Jefferson to have the US ships seize all vessels and goods that belonged to the Pasha and anything else deemed necessary. As they saw the US was actually committed to the fight, Algiers and

Tunis quickly abandoned the war and allegiance to Tripoli. Obviously, the US won the war. In fact, this was the reason why the line "to the shores of Tripoli" was added to the Marine Corps hymn. (Young Conservatives,, Joshua Riddle; "Obama can learn a lot from Thomas Jefferson's response to Muslims in 1801)

However, the Treaty of 1801 did not settle the piracy. In 1807, Algiers again started taking American ships and sailors hostage. Due to the War of 1812, it was not possible for the Americans to end the piracy. By 1815, America entered the Second Barbary War with a victory that led to treaties ending all tribute payments.

An interesting aside is found in the book *What Every American Needs To Know About The Qur'an*, by William Federer page 174:

Mohammad said "Whoever changes his Islamic religion, kill him." Thomas Jefferson owned a Qur'an to understand the enemy. He sent Marines to capture Tripoli... The Muslim terrorist attacks were stopped; giving rise to the Marine Anthem "From the Halls of Montezuma to the shores of Tripoli..." The curved Marine sword is from the confiscated Muslim scimitars, called "mamluke" swords. Marines are called "Leathernecks" for the wide leather straps worn around their necks to prevent being beheaded, as Sura 47 states, "When you meet the infidel in the battlefield, strike off their heads." The Turk's slaughter of Armenians, a Christian country, in 1915 horrified the entire civilized world. In a year and a half, the Islam militants killed 1.5 million Armenians, 750,000 Syrians, and a million others who they considered enemies of Islam. The USA and countries in Europe and Asia objected strenuously to this raging terror but never did a thing to stop the slaughter.[1]

Today an equally brutal Islam slaughter, cutting off heads, burning people alive, rape and every conceivable brutality perpetrated on Christians is taking place in the Middle East. All civilized nations

---

[1] (The History of Armenian Genocide, by Vahaku Dadrian)

look on in horror and, as was the case in 1915, the civilized world does nothing to stop it. An absolutely amazing repeat of history!

The above is discussed because Christianity continues to come under attack. Today Iran and the Islam terrorists have a goal of destroying Israel and "the Great Satin," the United States. Like Jefferson, it is wise to be fully aware of the enemy and recognize the horrors being committed in the Middle East every day, recognizing them as forecasts of their plans for us when the opportunity arises.

Chaplains are Part of a Team Effort

A team composed of the camp doctor, a command representative, a member of the military police, and the chaplain give an indoctrination seminar for newly arrived troops. The troops are welcomed aboard and given basic information about the camp, the services available, and basic information on base operations. The doctor discusses managing their health needs and allows a portion of his talk to mention dangers of being inflicted with venereal disease from prostitutes and like travelers. The military police point out the need for sobriety and the dangers of drunken driving, stressing safety is a byword in all military commands. The chaplain identifies the religious programs, encourages them to practice their faith, and assures them there is a reservoir of assistance available to them for managing personal or family situations. Like the others, he spends some time on controlled personal behavior, avoiding drugs, drinking booze to excess, and driving while drunk. He reminds them prostitutes can give them a moment of satisfaction and a lifetime of pain. Then he offers the chapel as a quiet home where God lives and welcomes visitors 24 hours a day. Most listen and find the admonitions acceptable for consideration. Some don't, and eventually I will see them again in the brig listening to them explain how fate "did them wrong."

Although almost all of them are in their teens or early twenties, a rather small number of them will marry and live in base housing. Somehow they manage to meet expenses and become an active member of the families in the housing area. Occasionally, trouble will arise, causing friction and anger. Generally, the problems arise because of immaturity, difficulty managing finances, or accepting bad advice as valid; and mom or dad is no longer there to evaluate the position. Chaplains have traditionally been the parental substitute. When marriage problems are involved, he becomes a third party who listens carefully to the situations festering in their relationships and gives his opinion without taking sides with either party. Although the resolution may be painful to one party, it is based on a great deal of experience and totally without prejudice.

Personnel new to the service exercise their newly found freedom from parental and other authorities who gave them guidance prior to leaving home to join the Armed Forces. They will have strict discipline in military matters, but their independence and self-discipline will govern their actions in other areas of their lives. The chaplain plays a significant role guiding them toward a life with rules and self-discipline as operating principles. If they run into trouble, it will generally take place outside the main gate where they will encounter illegal drugs, alcohol, prostitution, and relationships dragging them into unacceptable living conditions. The chaplain is the authority for guiding their personal lives back to a morally acceptable life. He helps them make difficult choices and to make a strong attachment to the value system God has given us for centuries.

As a Catholic chaplain I offered Mass daily and twice on Sundays. Confessions were heard before masses and whenever someone wanted to use this sacrament. Baptisms were administered after Mass or at some other times convenient to the parents. Adults who became Catholic completed a series of instructions given over a period of time, much like the RCIA programs presently used in civilian parishes. For those receiving the Sacrament of Confirmation, I would have them attend a Confirmation ceremony at a local parish and on one occasion we had a joint Marine and Army Confirmation ceremony at the Barstow Marine Base.

Other sacraments were given when appropriate. Pre-marital instructions were required for Catholics preparing for the sacrament. The courses were designed to instruct the couple in matters of faith. In addition to the faith instructions my training program included talks by a doctor on the physical issues of marriage such as abortion, respect for each other's needs, understanding the difficulties of pregnancy, etc.

A layman would also give instructions on the practical matters of married life, managing finances, educating the children in the faith, understanding and respecting interests of their spouses, and resolving differences with respect for each other. My part stressed the need for them to practice the faith in their daily lives and how this is done, the importance of living the faith daily, and making prayer an important part of their daily lives. The need to make arrangements to receive the sacraments frequently was a major concern of my message. I believe each of these programs is important, as each of them have positive effects on their live in the military and are necessary in a successful married life.

When children are brought into that relationship, they are to be accepted and raised as God's children, having them baptized and trained in their faith. There will be times when the children's actions make it seem as if the devil has taken control, but patience and a constant display of love for them helps their haloes reappear—at times still stained a bit. For a lot of reasons, both scholastic and religious, it is advisable to send them to a Catholic school. However, we are all aware of the cost involved in attendance at a Catholic school. In many cases, military families would have great difficulty meeting the Catholic school tuition. But the obligation to raise the children in the faith continues. Parish training programs attempt to fulfill the training requirement. To receive this training, the parents must ensure their children attend the classes faithfully. An important part of the training was dedicated to encouraging them to use the sacraments and develop the habit of a family praying together.

Often, premarital and information classes resulted in baptism and the reception of the sacraments. When premarital instructions were completed, I would notify the pastor of the parish where the marriage was to take place to confirm the person has completed the training. The instruction served to emphasize that marriage is a serious step deserving appropriate, constructive preparation for a lifelong experience. Individual instructions were given when a person was unable to attend classes. It is important for both the Catholic and non-Catholic parties to understand and accept the responsibilities of living a healthy family life.

Chapter 8
Specific Events During My Tour

In an attempt to clarify the type of activities in which the chaplain is involved, I have prepared several vignettes involving my life as a Navy Catholic chaplain. Other chaplains have had similar experiences, but I can only speak to those in which I was involved.

Misunderstandings arise because of absences or expressions improperly stated in correspondence with family or girlfriends that cannot be clarified at long distances. An example happened while I was attached to the *Shangri-La*, home ported in Mayport, Florida.

Ken, one of our sailors in his early 30s, married a lady about his same age. It was a very happy, well-managed marriage in all visible aspects. Six months or so after their marriage, Ken was transferred to a ship for a nine month tour. He really loved his wife and missed her every day. Toward the end of his tour, he was anxious to be with her again and wrote her a letter telling her how he wanted to have sex with her when he returned home. Ninety percent of the letter discussed some very intimate relationships he was dreaming of performing with her when his ship finally docked in Mayport. In today's world, this letter would probably be on the internet with a warning not to let children read it.

However, in this case, she was a dignified lady. She read the letter and found it disgusting. Shortly thereafter, she arrived at my office in tears. She entered my office and closed the door. I asked her to take a chair and tell me why she was so upset. She started to explain the situation and began to cry again. She handed me the letter she had received from her husband and asked me to read it. The letter was very expressive and a little crude, but clearly describing his intentions with very little concern about the way he expressed himself. The entire letter was about how much he loved her and about the sexual actions they would have together. I read the letter, folder it back up, placed it back in the envelope and returned it to her.

She took the letter, looked up at me and said, "How could he write me a disgusting letter like this?" I thought for a minute and replied, "Linda, you did not marry Shakespeare or John Keats. You married Ken; a sailor who obviously loves you dearly but expressed his love in a very physical manner. His heart is all over this letter. He misses you terribly and can hardly wait to take you in his arms again and share his life with you. There are dozens of wives who would love to receive a letter like this telling them their husbands want to be home with them, sharing their love like he had expressed."

I told her about a sailor who visited my office asking what he could do to save his marriage. His wife found being married to him an impossible burden and now found it necessary to divorce him. She's a thousand miles away and found even that distance too close. No children were involved, but this request for a divorce brought an end to a life he truly loved; his personal life had just crashed. He would have loved to receive a letter like this from her, regardless of how she would express herself telling him she missed being held by him and expressing their love sexually.

We discussed the letter for a while and she left, hopefully reevaluating the grammatical style he chose to express his love for her. I often wondered if she gave him some English lessons on use of less earthy adjectives. I knew Ken, a tough, physical man who was always absolutely loyal to her. I never saw either of them again. But I believe the marriage is still strong and their lives together a happy union.

Daddy, Please Don't Kill Us!

This particular Wednesday started as did any other Wednesday, a clear sky and a warm breeze. Flora Whiting left her trailer home about 10:00 o'clock for her weekly trip to the base commissary. Flora usually did her weekly grocery shopping at the base commissary around the middle of the week. There were fewer shoppers, giving her time to select items on her shopping list and check for additions made since her last visit.

She stepped out of her trailer home making sure the door was locked. Her hand rested lightly on the straps of her purse as she approached the Carlos Coronado family trailer. The Coronado's were close friends. Their children spent their free time playing together, much of which included time spent in each of their homes. This morning as she passed the Coronado home sounds of children crying caught her attention. She thought this was rather strange. She wondered why the kids were not in school. As she walked past the trailer's front door, she looked at their trailer, trying to see what was happening. The main door was open but the screen door was closed, making it impossible to see clearly any figures moving inside the home. This was also unfamiliar, as the Coronado kids were full of energy and would more likely be running around the trailer, certainly not just standing still staring at something she could not see.

Then she heard children crying and begging their dad *not to kill them*. At first she thought this could not be happening in the Coronado family, so it was probably a TV program. But she had real doubts because the voices sounded like the Coronado children. After listening carefully for a time, she knew it was *not* the TV. The voices she heard were those of real children. The voice of the oldest daughter, Maria, was distinct as she begged her dad, "Please daddy, don't kill me. I love you daddy, please don't kill me." The others were sobbing and begging their dad not to shoot them.

For a moment she stood frozen. Although not visible, she knew Nicole, their mother, was terrified. Realizing the calls for help were really coming from the Coronado wife and children, begging Carlos, the dad, not to kill them. It was happening in real time. She recognized the voice of their youngest son who played with her son and were in and out of both houses several times a day; she did not know if others were in the house. She heard Nicole telling her husband, "Carlos, why are you doing this? Please, put down the gun."

Her thoughts were now totally absorbed in the danger being faced by the family. The need to find help flashed before her mind. She had no doubt Carlos was about to kill his family. The cries sent chills down her spine. Knowing there was no way she could intervene without becoming a victim herself or make the situation worse, she realized it was up to her to find someone to stop this disaster. She hurried back to her trailer, grabbed the phone, and called my office. Both families were Catholic, and she felt perhaps Father could stop this from happening.

When I answered the phone, she was frantic. "Father, I just walked past the Coronado trailer, and I heard Nicole and the kids begging Carlos not to kill them! The threats are real. I am sure Carlos is threatening to kill his wife and children. The front door to their trailer was open, and I heard the children sobbing and crying, begging their father not to kill them! Father, they are really scared; I know he is going to kill them if someone does not stop him! Please, Father, you have to go there now! Sarge has a gun, and it sounds like he is crazy, ready to use it to kill his family. Please hurry; maybe you can stop him! Dear God, a mass murder on our base... Please hurry!" I agreed and thanked her for making the call.

Flora was right. Carlos seemed to be deranged, preparing to murder his own wife and children. I realized if someone could kill his own family, he would have no compunction about killing others. I called security and asked to have a detail sent to the area. If I could not stop the killing or be taken out with the family, they would be in a position to step in and resolve the crisis before he would leave the trailer and harm others living in base housing. I gave them the information I had, telling them Carlos has a weapon and was about to use it. His wife and kids are crying, begging him not to shoot them. I asked to have a security detail sent to the area in the event I was not able to stop him or did not come out of it alive.

Not knowing the cause of this problem, I realized my appearance at his doorway dressed in a Marine officer uniform could increase his anger and make my entrance into the next life a little earlier than I planned. To decrease this possibility, I took off my officer's uniform and changed into my civilian priest's garb – a black suit, white collar, etc. – before driving to the scene. I always kept a set of civilian dress in my office for any number of reasons. In this case, I wanted to make sure the sergeant saw the black suit and roman collar of a Catholic priest walking toward him and not a security guard coming to take serious disciplinary action. As I walked up the path, I said a prayer asking God to resolve this matter peacefully before this family was destroyed.

Reaching the trailer, I found the front door open and the screen closed. Although the screen door hindered my ability to see clearly into the trailer, I could hear crying and muffled words of some very frightened people. Security wasted no time. When I reached the trailer, they were already there, weapons drawn. One was hiding behind a tree near the front of the trailer while another was pushed up against the far end of the trailer. There were probably others at the ready, but I did not see them.

Peering through the screen door, I could see a dark image of the family huddled together in the middle of the living room. It looked like the sergeant still had the weapon in his hand. I quietly opened the screen door and entered the trailer. On the floor in the middle of the living room Carlos' wife and children were hugging together, crying, and the sergeant was saying "I'm so sorry, I am so very sorry. We are going to lose everything."

Quietly, a Marine security officer, who entered the trailer after me, came up behind me, reached over my shoulder, and retrieved the .45 caliber weapon from the sergeant's hand. Carlos had no reluctance to give it up. As I knelt down next to them, I prayed this problem would be solved peacefully.

When the sergeant regrouped, I asked him, "Sarge, what the hell happened to you? Why would you threaten the lives of Nicole and the kids?" He answered. "Father, I owe $10,000 on this trailer. On my income, I have no way to keep up with the payments, feed my family, or buy clothes for my kids. The problem is getting worse, and I have no way to keep up. I have nowhere to go for help."

I told him he wasn't alone. "All of us have a mortgage on our homes and many other expenses everyone has to meet. Sarge," I said, "there are other families living on this base with problems just like yours, but killing their families is not a solution." Before I could discuss the problem further, security personnel had him cuffed and out of the trailer. As the incident ended, a solution to the problem seemed bleak at best.

As he left, I thought to myself that this crisis was over but the problem continues to exist and is now exacerbated. What was the family going to do without his support? Suddenly housing, food, clothing, and attendance at school became major issues. Resolving the immediate crisis was necessary, but it failed to manage the real problem – married couples supporting a family on an income barely meeting everyday expenses. Problems like this can quickly overtake the family's ability to manage their financial matters. Most of the time, managing a debt like this pulls them together, strengthens and matures the marriage. However, exceptions do happen, as it did in this case.

One organization with a history of assisting in matters like this is the Navy League. But even the League has limits governing their operations. They are not set up for "long haul" assistance. In most such cases, a family manages the crisis by turning to their immediate family for support and assistance in meeting daily needs. When these are not available, seeking resolution can rapidly become a tragedy. At times there are sources available to assist, but when that is not available, some real suffering takes place as they attempt to restore normality in their lives.

Later in the day, I returned to my home, wondering what would happen to this family. The Navy League had been contacted and the command was aware of the events and their resolution. What will happen to this family as it seeks a source of income and a way to raise children without a dad? I thought of those killed in action and the burdens impacting their families. In a matter of minutes, a normal life is drastically changed as his wife and children must now accept the loss and meet the financial burdens awaiting them after the loss of a husband and dad.

A case as severe as this one doesn't happen every day. But situations like this do take place. When they do, the chaplain is called to help resolve the issues, attempt to get the problem under control, and assist the family to make changes as circumstances dictate. At times, an incident like this can absorb the chaplain's time for several hours, days, or longer. Chaplains are a part of military families and often serve as an ombudsman to manage personnel issues seriously impacting the lives of military personnel. The chaplain's main duty is to manage the spiritual needs of military personnel and their families. But, like pastors in civilian parishes, his job includes assisting wherever the need arises.

Life In The Military Is A Maturing Process

As mentioned earlier, the average age of military personnel is 19, and like non-military 19 year olds they experience the same problems encountered by those in their later teens adjusting to the demands of becoming an adult. The major difference between military personnel and their counter parts in civilian life are the serious responsibilities military personnel encounter upon entering the service. They find themselves responsible for multi-million dollar aircraft, highly classified electronic systems, and driving armored tanks with almost unimaginable fire power. Even more demanding is the responsibility for the troops with whom they are stationed and who depend on them to cover their backs as they move out to neutralize some objective.

The necessity of learning to control their fear and continue their actions, regardless of the sweat and anxiety that would otherwise send them running for cover, is at times a part of their lives. While all this is happening, they have personal concerns smothered for the moment yet continuing to demand resolution. Problems at home are exacerbated by their absence—meeting financial obligations with a restricted income and boyfriends/girlfriends issues pull for their attention at times, causing depression or serious anger. These and dozens of other problems vie for attention and resolution. Many of these cannot be managed without help. It is also in this arena that chaplains become the person to approach for assistance. Their training, experience and access to authorities most often allow him to find resolutions to both military and personal problems.

One of the Marines serving overseas may receive a letter from his wife requesting a divorce. During his absence, his wife met and fell in love with another man and has decided to marry him in the immediate future. The Marine is serving overseas and is unable to manage the problem personally. The complications involved in a matter like this will absorb his life, affecting both his work and personal life. When children are involved, the situation is exacerbated.

A wife may write a letter telling her husband that their 16 year old daughter is pregnant or their eldest son is having difficulties at school and won't listen to her. She tells him she is sick and tired of being both father and mother to the children. If he is in Iraq or on a cruise in the

Mediterranean, or serving in Okinawa or Germany, he is unable to return and attempt to resolve the issues plaguing his family. He needs some help and is generally unable to discuss the problem with those he works with. The chaplain becomes the major player who can listen and attempt to find some resolution to relieve the stress he is experiencing including finding assistance stateside when such is appropriate.

A child may be found to have serious health problems such as cancer, requiring constant attention of the parent. One of the children may have a behavior problem and is disrupting the family. The parent at home is unable to control the child and his association with rude, undisciplined gang-like-thugs is making matters worse. Financial problems affecting rent payments, credit status, purchase of supplies for the children at school, and a dozen other matters affected by this problem are pressuring him to pay his bills.

Problems like these and dozens of other like situations tear at a person's heart, seriously impact his life and affecting his job performance. To help settle his anxieties, he has to talk with someone. Talking with the chaplain may not resolve all issues, but it will give him a chance to share the problem in keeping with the proverb, "A problem shared is a problem halved." At times, problems can make a person's inner life a miserable world. Very often sharing problems with a third party can make an evaluation with "a new set of eyes" unencumbered by relationships that may contaminate the resolution process.

Being attached to a base stateside operates much like a civilian parish. Many of the families with children send them to a local Catholic School. Others send their children to public schools. In this case, the parents have the responsibility to teach their children the faith, and they attend catechism classes given by the local parish. In addition, following the end of the school year the base chaplain would have summer classes specifically designed to prepare military children for First Communion and Confirmation. When the troops are stationed stateside, their lives are normalized with activities like those that make up the lives of non-military families. It also proved a great benefit for the Catholic chaplain who manages to get an occasional invite to supper and a decent evening meal!

Separation, a Major Military Characteristic

A major characteristic in military life is separation from families. Navy personnel assigned to sea duty experience several months or years, depending on engagements, in which he may be away. Everyone understands when you enter the armed services there will be separations from family members. Recruits' initial training program will last several weeks. However, once trained, assignments often include duty stations where families cannot follow for any number of reasons. Mediterranean cruise sailors find the ship constantly at sea for a tour of duty lasting 7-12 months—or longer. Marines discover that their assignments take them overseas to stations where families cannot relocate, as is the case in a transfer to Okinawa where they will spend a year. Assignments like these take place under normal circumstances. When situations like Vietnam or the Middle East conflicts take place, separations can involve several long, trying tours away from their families.

This is especially true in our time. Our Armed Forces are now being seriously reduced in size, forcing situations that require troops to be called back to duty for months, as their skills are required. Fathers or mothers need help to discipline their children and make daily household decisions and share matters vital to the success or failure of a family. Carrying on alone calls for deep commitment on the part of the wife and husband.

At times, serious problems arise where the spouse cannot assist in their resolution. The military person is not just a sailor or Marine. S/he is a whole person who lives in the military and is simultaneously a family member. Problems in the lives of the military family can impact their whole person at times with unfortunate results.

So many of the disagreements concern money and how it is to be controlled. The wife, at home, has to account for all expenditures, carefully avoiding purchases beyond their financial capacity. Rent, food, and clothing consumes nearly all of their income. The Marine or sailor wants his wife to find an outside job to help defray some of the costs that must be met every day. She objects because her life is filled with caring for the children, making meals, washing clothes, helping the children with their homework and cleaning the house. At times, children fail to realize the place is a home and not a shed or barn.

Another much more difficult problem to resolve happens when a third party enters the scene, straining their relationship. This change in attitude is not lost on the children. Becoming aware of the changed relations, they react with fear and sometimes anger, upsetting the entire family. The hurt they feel may go unnoticed, even though their insides are being torn apart. The fighting and quarrelling may hurt them, but they can learn to live with controlled behavior. Divorce leaves the children in a world where they believe parental love does not exist and their sense of self-worth is shattered, often leaving the children believing they are the real cause of the separation.

When involved in family disputes, I felt it was my duty to keep the family together if at all possible. I always thanked God situations like this seldom took place. An interesting fact is the experience teachers have with children of families where divorce is under way. Children who were well behaved, happy, and a part of everyday school life become angry, get into fights, and are constantly upset. Even though there has been no word of a divorce in the works, the teacher knows immediately the children are reacting to an approaching marriage breakup.

Military families function with an understanding that separation is a necessary part of their lives. As mentioned above, discussing problems openly and honestly allows the couple to encounter the real issues at the heart of the struggle. This approach works as they discover neither of them knew what was really bothering them, with remarks like, "Well, I didn't know that; I thought (whatever her /his understanding was)." Counseling allows us to identify the actual problem, and in most cases brings about an understanding that relieves the tension between the parties. This process clarifies the matter and allows for changes necessary to resolve the problem to the satisfaction of both parties. The obvious conclusion is that the parties did not take time to discuss openly the problem with each other. Counseling leads to a reasonable resolution in their lives together.

I recall a case in Pensacola when a couple came in to discuss getting a divorce. They introduced themselves, sat down, and started telling me their marriage was in shambles. They believed their differences could not be resolved and should end in a divorce. As the conversation between them progressed, I heard several comments such as, "I didn't know that," and, "Why didn't you tell me?" and, "I thought you…" I did almost nothing but be a good listener. When they had thoroughly evaluated the issues themselves, they thanked me for helping them and left my office smiling. The idea of a divorce faded away. Years later, I met them at a bowling alley. When their rounds were completed, they came over and thanked me for saving their marriage. I responded by saying, "I'm glad everything worked out OK," and saying to myself I didn't do anything. However, our experience tells us not all marital problems end well.

Problems like these can absorb a great deal of the chaplain's time. But like so many other duties affecting the lives of military personnel, the chaplain's time is spent assisting troops to manage many areas, spiritual and other forces impacting their lives.

Chapter 9
Camp Pendleton, California - First Assignment

The 1st Marine Division–5th Battalion, stationed in Camp Pendleton, California, was my first assignment. The 5th Marines, Camp Margarita, an infantry battalion, had the honor of being one of the country's most decorated military units, with a rich history of successful combat engagements. I was about to discover Marines are in constant preparation for combat with training that is deadly serious. Training absorbs their life. They develop a respect for the weapons they use and give attention to the maintenance required to keep them fully operational. An unspoken but very real commitment to excellence permeates their activities.

War is always serious business as is staying alive. The need for intense training is obvious, centering on physical and mental development and an understanding of the construction and use of their weapons. Of equal importance is learning they are part of a combat unit whose survival is totally dependent on their unified efforts. To keep themselves alive, it is essential to give their best efforts to protect the lives of the rest of their unit. The development of weapons skills and the need to carry out their assignments with excellence develops the confidence needed to make them an effective member of a combat team. This interdependence is fostered as they train together and gradually learn their personal survival is dependent on other members of their outfit.

Participating in Marine Train Programs

To be an effective member of my Marine Corps assignments, I believed it necessary to participate in as many of their training programs as I was allowed. Some were exhausting, like a 20 mile hike; some were fun, like firing weapons at a shooting range. One exercise generated a real concern because its detonation was generated ten seconds after a pin was pulled. Specifically, I am referring to a grenade. There is a ten second delay from the time the pin is pulled and the explosion occurs. Believing the time delay is accurately installed calls for great trust in the folks manufacturing it!

The hand grenade is about the size of a baseball. There is always the concern the timing device was not working correctly and it would explode in less than 10 seconds. Eventually you accept the fact the mechanism does work as designed and will not explode before the 10 seconds have passed. This sense of trust carries over to all the equipment used by the troops. I remember during a flight sitting next to a paratrooper discussing trust in the parachute opening when the rip cord is pulled. His response was matter-of-fact and confident. He answered, "The chute always opens". That is the same kind of trust present when holding and throwing a hand grenade.

I recall one episode involving throwing hand grenades. The practice was carried out in a cement cubicle about six feet by six feet in diameter with walls around eight feet high; high enough for the average sized person to not see over the top of the structure.

The grenade is an anti-personnel fragmentation weapon. It is designed to explode sometime after it had been triggered. The grenade we used had a 10 second delay from the time you pulled the pin until it exploded. This allowed sufficient time to ignite the weapon and throw it out of the structure where the trainee and his instructor are standing. The technique we used was to pull the pin and throw it over hand to the ground outside our shelter. A few seconds later the grenade would explode with sufficient force to kill or seriously injure anyone in the area of the explosion.

There were stories of a trainee pulling the ring out of the grenade and dropping it to the ground, where it exploded before it could be picked up and thrown over the wall. This kind of explosion would kill both the trainee and the instructor. I am not aware of any such incident actually taking place wherever I was stationed.

Finding Living Quarters

Until I was able to find off-base housing, I rented a room at a motel on the beach at Oceanside, California. This proved to be a great decision. The motel was close to the beach, allowing me to hear the sound of waves rushing up the shoreline as if to catch a prize and then easing back down to the water's edge, admitting a failed effort. This continuing action proved to be a relaxing experience. Every evening, about 5:00 pm, a light, cool breeze would emerge from the ocean, move across the beach into the city, and go on to the Rocky Mountains, which formed a barrier at times and preventing the breeze from reaching communities beyond the east side of the mountains. Additionally, renting by the week I was given a much-reduced rate. An unexpected benefit was a 24-hour phone answering service and a change of bedding twice a week. The motel also had a laundry room available to all residents.

A memorable feature of the motel's location was the historic Oceanside Pier, the longest wooden pier on the West Coast, stretching 1,942 feet into the Pacific Ocean. A cool breeze made walking on the pier a comfortable, relaxing experience. Living so close to the Pacific Ocean gave us an average weather temperature of 69 degrees, and a pier available for fishing and long walks made the motel an ideal living location.

I reported aboard the base on the date assigned and took over the duties of a Navy Catholic chaplain at Camp Margarita, a Marine Infantry base. Before I met the commanding officer, I met Father Sporer, a retired Navy chaplain living in Oceanside, California. He knew the commanding officer, the Sergeant Major, and several other personnel. He went with me to the base and introduced me to the commanding officer. I spent the rest of the day visiting base facilities and introducing myself to some of the troops. Before leaving the base, I spent some time at the base chapel organizing my office.

John Condit, the Catholic chaplain stationed at the northern most Marine base, Camp Onofre, rented a house in San Clemente. He invited me to join him at his residence and share rent and utility costs. It was large enough to allow two of us to live there comfortably. I transferred my personal gear and equipment to this address and operated out of this residence for the rest of my stay in Camp Pendleton. Living in San Clemente had many advantages, one of which is the shortened distance to Camp Margarita. The house had a garden in the back yard with a variety of flowers filling the air with a pleasant aroma. My quarters were in the rear of the building. I had the back bedroom with a sliding door I kept open all night. Each morning I would wake up with the fragrance of flowers filling my room. I will never forget the extraordinarily wonderful living conditions I had in San Clemente.

John had a great sense of humor. His mother was in show business and his dad was a protestant minister. He was occasionally asked how they ever met and eventually married. One day I had an opportunity to attend an introduction class he was giving to newly arrived Marines. He introduced himself with the following: "I'm Father John Condit from Missouri – where the men are men and the sheep are nervous." This always received a great response while relaxing the troops and capturing their attention. Then he discussed moral and personal issues they would encounter in military life. He always reminded the troops it was necessary to approach their lives as adults with a mature sense of morality and responsibility.

John was a great cook. Occasionally he would have guests for dinner and prepare meals so special the wives were concerned about inviting him to dinner, afraid they would not be able to compete. Living in the same house, I was able to join in the conversations and enjoy the dinners with the guests. This opportunity came with a small price. My participation involved cleanup activities following the meal, washing dishes, pots and pans and cleaning up the kitchen. It was a small price to enjoy the company and partake of his outstanding meals!

We both had Wednesday off since our weekends were filled with offering Mass and managing other liturgical functions. Almost every Wednesday, we took a trip to some interesting historical site in Southern California. Most often we would end our trip by driving to Los Angeles and taking in a play at a theatre, have dinner at a pizza restaurant, and then return to San Clemente.

Generally, I would do the driving on the return trip. Driving home often proved to be dangerous. Fog from the ocean would settle over Highway 101 so thickly there were times I could not see the lane markings on the pavement. (At times we would refer to Highway 101 as "Highway 10 to 1 you don't make it.") All I could do was watch the red tail lights of the car in front of me. It was important to stay rather close enough to the car ahead of me because failing to do so would leave us without a guide to follow. Should this happen, I would have had no way to determine where the road was. Should one of them have gone over the side, we would have become a part of the wreckage! Every so often the fog would lift up, clearing the air and allowing us to see the road and the countryside. When this happened we could see a long stream of cars ahead of us, driving the same way we were, very carefully. When we entered the fog again, staying close to the car ahead of us was absolutely necessary.

I looked forward to making these trips with John. His knowledge of this part of California allowed us to select sites with historical significance or famous for some special importance like the Huntington Gardens or the studios in Hollywood.

In a recent trip to Los Angeles and Camp Pendleton, I found the world I knew smothered by tall buildings, multiple freeways and crowds of people hurrying to reach some very important destinations. The relaxed atmosphere I knew had disappeared and was replaced by loud music, car horns, and busy people who seemed unable or unwilling to stop and smell the roses. My memories of Los Angeles and Camp Pendleton and parts of Southern California as I knew them continue to be memories I cherish to this day.

Marines Constantly Train For Combat

As mentioned above, working with an infantry division made me aware of just how serious the Marines are about training. The troops are trained in the use and maintenance of their weapons and the care and use of the electronic and mechanical equipment integral to Marine operating systems.

The major skill troops develop is to function as a disciplined unit, with common objectives. Lessons like this cannot be taught in a classroom. They are developed over months of training as they encounter situations demanding cooperation with other Marines or experience a failed program. Each of them became aware of the need to be self-disciplined, fully capable of performing tasks assigned to them. Understanding how a unit functions when in combat is vital for all troops as there are occasions when any one of them could become responsible for commanding a unit.

One example takes place when a commander of a unit is killed or severely injured and left unable to manage his troops. Our forces are organized so the next highest ranking person automatically takes over command of the unit, giving it discipline and unity of actions. This process helps to ensure the mission remains the objective and leadership remains the fundamental quality required throughout the ranks of the Marine Corps. Any Marine may end up in a leadership role, responsible for his life and those of the troops in his unit.

A Long Hike

On a Wednesday afternoon, I was introduced to one of the battalion's training programs with a phone call from the Commanding officer around 3:30 pm telling me I was to join the battalion with a full field pack on a 20 mile hike *tomorrow* morning at 7:00 am. Twenty miles was more walking than I would do in a week. However, at 7:00 am I was present and ready to go. Once the troops were organized, we began to move out. I joined the skipper toward the end of the line. We were followed by a jeep with a medical unit. Given the size of our battalion, it took a while before our headquarters unit actually began to move. When we began the march, the sun was out and the weather was great.

We had completed about an hour when a Marine exhausted from carrying a mortar plate fell into a ditch about four feet below the level of the road. He struggled to get up, but it looked like he had encountered an impossible task. We were about 20 or so feet behind him, so I helped him up and carried the mortar plate for a short time, perhaps 10 minutes, until he was able to take it back. He reached over and took the plate back and thanked me for the assistance. When I got back in my position, I asked how much the plate weighed and was told it weighed in at 40 lbs. At first I thought that weight couldn't be right because when I carried it I thought a ton would be a more accurate evaluation. When the Marine took back the plate, he completed the rest of the march without any obvious difficulty.

About half way through the march, we stopped for a short rest and a bit of food. At this point, I was beginning to feel the strain of walking this distance. When we began to move out again, the commander and some headquarters personnel officers and I moved to the head of the line.

A basic factor takes place when moving in a long line of Marines. Not everyone on the line starts moving at the same time. Those in front start and others begin to follow at a slightly later time, etc. As a result, the line begins to extend so people at the end of the line at times had to run to catch up and after they reach the people in front them; the line would stop and then start again for the entire march. Walking in front of the line had definite benefits.

By the time we had walked for about 18 of the 20 miles, we could see Camp Margarita and the end of the march. However, at some distance in front of us I could see a rather high, steep hill in our path. I believed I could make it to the camp if we walked around it but had real doubts about making it to the top of the hill. As we were climbing, the skipper looked at me and said, "Just keep putting one foot in front of the other." This advice proved true and became a principle that governed my judgments for the rest of my life.

"When things get tough, don't quit, just keep putting one foot ahead of the other to reach your goal." No sooner had we started down the camp-side of the hill, we saw the Marine Corps band at a distance playing the Marine Corps hymn. We all stopped, squared away our gear, regrouped, and marched into camp with all the vigor we could muster.

When we broke ranks, I got in my car and drove home starving and fully exhausted. I made a ham and cheese sandwich, took a can of beer out of the refrigerator, and went to take a hot bath. When I took off my boots, my feet swelled up to a size where I would not have been able to put them back on. I managed to step into the tub filled with hot water and sit down. I took a bite of the sandwich and a sip of beer from the can, rested them on the edge of the tub and leaned on the back. In a matter of seconds I fell sound asleep. Several hours later I woke up, the bath water was cold, the beer was warm, and I was still starving!

Chapter 10
Cuban Crisis

During this period, our relations with Cuba and the Soviet Union had been strained for a long time. The Bay of Pigs fiasco further embittered Cuba, encouraging it to use their closeness to our borders as a launching pad for Soviet nuclear weapons. The project was started. Nuclear weapons were introduced to the island and prepared to be fired at the U.S., and President Kennedy had to take actions necessary to force the Soviet Union to remove the weapons.

Both parties, Russia and Cuba, refused to comply with our requests to remove the weapons. Our only option was to make preparations for an invasion of Cuba to remove the weapons ourselves. Our military forces were called into action and preparations were made to invade Cuba. All Marine units were called to return to base and prepare to board troop ships for the move to the US Naval Base at Guantanamo Bay, located on the east coast of Cuba.

When this notification took place, I was shopping in San Clemente. A helicopter flew over the city with a loud speaker telling all Marines to return to their bases immediately. I drove home, packed my gear, and hurried to Camp Margarita. When I left the camp to drive home, there were no signs along the road indicating combat readiness was underway. Following our directive to return to base, I drove the same road back to Camp Margarita and was amazed at the volume of ammunition stacked on pallets alongside the base highway. I wondered where all this ammo came from and who arranged it in perfect order for removal by the truckload. There were miles of ammunition ready for loading on supply ships harbored in Long Beach, California.

Shortly after I arrived at Camp Margarita, officers were briefed on the Cuban Crisis that had developed because of Russia's installation of nuclear missiles with the capacity of striking US cities. President Kennedy threatened to invade Cuba unless the missiles were removed from Cuba and wanted the Russians to cease their involvement in our hemisphere. An invasion of Cuba by our Armed Forces was set in motion. A threat of this magnitude had to be eliminated permanently, and our action to ensure the elimination of the missiles took place immediately.

Sunday morning, our battalion moved out of Camp Margarita to Long Beach California, where we boarded a ship for the trip to Cuba. I had two Masses to offer on Sunday morning before I could join the troops in Long Beach. When I finished the 10 o'clock Mass, a driver was waiting to take me to the ship. By this time my clerk had prepared my totally squared away backpack. I gathered my gear and took the trip to Long Beach.

By the time I arrived, our troops were already onboard prepared to move out. When I neared the ship I received a lot of "cat calls" claiming I didn't prepare my own backpack and that it was in too good a shape to be my work. I yelled back, "You're crazy, I did it myself." Of course they did not believe me, as I knew they wouldn't. I joined a group of Marines watching ships being loaded with supplies, ammunition and vehicles. All the Marine personnel were already onboard. I joined a group of them on the main deck watching the activities taking place on the docks and waiting for our ship to move out. That evening we left port and began our trip to Cuban waters.

Trip to Cuba

We sailed south along the West Coast of the United States through the warm waters of the Pacific Ocean. A young marine officer, newly assigned to our outfit, and I stood on the main deck watching the bow of the ship create waves turning them into a spray of colors quickly slipping away to make way for others to follow. Dolphins, as if showing off their swimming style, followed us riding the wash created by the bow of our ship. We were amazed at their capacity to stay with us maintaining the speed of our ship. Warm water, a cool breeze and a softly lite moon slowly moving along its course took our minds off the horror to be faced in battles to be fought.

For a moment we enjoyed the comfort of a ship sailing south on a calm sea with a light breeze to counter the heat. As we drew near the Panama Canal I realized what an absolute marvel of engineering this navigation system was. From a distance it appeared we were too large to squeeze through the locks. However, as we entered them I was amazed how easily we moved into place even leaving space on either side of the ship; much like placing a hand in an oversized glove.

Just prior to entering the locks, a Marine received a message his brother had been killed in a car accident. He was asked to come home for the funeral. He had a close relationship with his younger brother but feared, given the mission we were on, his request for leave would not be granted. Under ordinary circumstances, without the possibility of a looming conflict with Cuba, there would be no problem allowing him to return home to his brother's funeral. He asked me to request leave for him, realizing since we were going into combat and the command might not approve his request. I believed it was worth a try, so I talked with the colonel, asking that the Marine be allowed to return home for the burial. At first he objected, reminding me we were not on a vacation cruise. However, he did grant the leave while we were passing through the locks, allowing the Marine to step off the ship and make arrangements for his trip home. While moving along the Panama Canal, another Marine became sick and was taken off the ship to a shore facility for treatment.

Although the cruise carried us through some really beautiful landscapes, the history of its construction was a reminder of the cost in human life lost in its construction.

Panama Canal Passage

The trip proved to be a cruise through a swamp with high humidity, uncomfortable heat, and thick green vegetation that spread in every direction. The Panama Canal cut through dense virgin jungle; a terrain which made developing the canal extremely difficult.

It was built at a great cost financially, with an enormous loss of human lives. The Panama Canal in 1914 cost Americans around $375,000,000, including the $10,000,000 paid to Panama and the $40,000,000 paid to the French company. It was the single most expensive construction project in United States history to that time. Fortifications cost extra, about $12,000,000. The actual costs in US dollars to construct the canal differ depending on the author and the research conducted. One of the more accepted figures is that of Noel Maurer and Carlos Yu who determined that the cost, in today's economy would be $119.4 billion. (What Roosevelt Took: The Economic Impact of the Panama Canal, 1903-37)

Not included in the price is the loss of life of those who died digging, running the railroad, and operating excavating equipment. Malaria, Yellow Fever, dysentery, Typhoid and Dengue took five hundred lives for every mile (fifty miles) of the length of the canal. During the construction period it was known as a "tropical pesthole" and as a "white man's grave." However, constructing the canal was four times more deadly for the black man than it was for the white.

The French worked at the site from 1881 to 1889, during which 22,000 workers were killed. When the US took over construction, 5,269 people lost their lives. The total death toll reached 27,269 workers. The work was so dangerous and took so many lives that the cost is difficult to calculate accurately. The work itself was dangerous by its very nature. The use or misuse of dynamite to blast away layers of soil and rock took hundreds of lives. Mishandling a box of dynamite would set off an explosion killing dozens of "power men" (men who carried 50 pound dynamite boxes on their heads and shoulders to the construction site.) Even their sweat on this highly unstable material was liable to set off an explosion, killing them and those near them! Many deaths were caused by railroad accidents. Hundreds lost their lives and limbs by falling off moving dirt cars and rail transportation. Funeral trains were legendary. Three times a day, those killed in accidents and those who died of disease were loaded on trains and taken out to mass burial sites. Deaths from disease remained consistently high until it was determined mosquitoes were spreading deadly diseases like Malaria. Once the mosquito abatement programs were installed, the death from disease was minimal.

With this information, my trip through the canal proved to be a visit to a huge burial ground. It was a serious reminder that the foundation for the conveniences we were experiencing rested on the bodies of thousands of men who made the Panama Canal a reality.

The practical nature of the canal makes it a most important strategic point of control. When President Carter gave it to the Panamanians, it felt like we were at the mercy of any country to whom they would sell its control. As it is now, China has control of the canal and all the traffic flowing through it. In the event we have serious problems with China, they could shut out our use of the canal, causing serious damage to our shipping lanes and the strength of our national defense. Perhaps this may not have been a wise decision over the long haul.

Guantanamo Bay

Upon completing our trip through the canal, the cooler weather of the Caribbean was appreciated. Approaching Guantanamo Bay, Cuba, we found the Atlantic Ocean waves appeared to be more frequent and choppy than those we encountered sailing on the Pacific Ocean.

Completing our trip through the canal and moving into Guantanamo Bay brought to mind the seriousness of the mission we were to encounter. We were not sure what part we were to play in the event of a conflict. The word we received was we were to be a helicopter landing team placed in the middle of the island; not the safest place to be on an island populated with a communist government.

Upon reaching Guantanamo Bay, we saw a Naval base with an airport overstuffed with aircraft, military equipment, and armed personnel. It looked like the base was too small to hold all the activities taking place with the people and equipment filling all the vacant spots. As we arrived at our station, we realized we had joined an armada of ships. The island airport was crowded with aircraft delivering combat personnel and supplies. Military personnel filled every corner of the base.

An interesting factor to consider was a one hundred foot cliff on the Cuban side of the Naval base allowing Cuban forces to observe operations taking place beneath them. It almost seemed like the Cubans could bring up some heavy equipment and do some real damage to the activities being carried out below them. However, Cuba could not arrange such an invasion since we were fully aware of their troop activities. Any attempt by them to invade the Naval base would make interesting reading in future history books as it would describe the massacre that took place when such an attack was met with the military strength of USA Armed Forces gathering on Guantanamo Naval Base. We could unleash its forces and remove Castro and his administration for the next several centuries. It didn't take deep thinking to determine such an action would be a disaster before they moved the first piece of equipment.

Arriving at Guantanamo Naval Station

Our Battalion did not disembark. In circumstances other than those involving actual combat, in which we were now engaged, the island could have been an outstanding location for a resort. The beaches were excellent, much like those found on the Gulf Coast of Florida.

It was difficult to see any great distance into the thick forest. The trees crowded out undergrowth found in wooded areas less developed than those surrounding us as we made our way down a gravel road to the beach. The forest had an aroma of fresh wild flowers carried by a clean refreshing breeze. Several hundred yards from our entrance to the forest, we came across a beach with soft white sand extending at least one hundred feet from the water's edge. I remember there were no rocks on the sand from the grass to the water. This beach looked like it could have been transported from Florida's Santa Rosa Island or Tampa Bay. It seemed to demand we use this opportunity to go for a swim. The water was warm, clean, and relaxing; free of the paper, plastic, bags, diapers and other debris often found on public beaches.

So, responding to this silent invitation, some of us stripped to our shorts and dove in. The water was comfortable, unaffected by a tide slowly making its way to the beach. I don't recall how long we stayed, but it was far less than I would have liked. But time demanded we return to the training taking place around us. Viegues frequently served as a firing range for weapons used by Navy ships. The sound of weapons and exploding ammo reminded us this was not a vacation cruise. When we left the beach, we returned to a shooting range to complete the day's exercise.

This is just an aside, but while on the Island of Viegues, I was given the opportunity to fire a fifty-caliber weapon at some barrels a hundred or so yards from our location. I hit them and credited this success to the days I spent hunting deer and birds in Northern

Michigan prior to entering the Navy. However, the officer evaluating the practice gave the credit to sheer luck. He was probably correct, but I like to believe my past hunting experiences had at least some influence on making a correct aim on the targets. For the rest of our stay in the Cuban waters, training continued.

Guantanamo Bay Naval Station is the only US Naval base on communist soil. It was a beautiful base where numerous admirals and other high-ranking officers would spend their twilight years, closing out their careers before retirement.

Ordinarily, problems in Cuba would be of little interest, but Cuba's relationship with us had become unfriendly. The situation became worse when Castro allowed the Soviets to build missile silos capable of sending nuclear weapons into mainland USA. This situation was unacceptable, and we were there to ensure the threat of Soviet missiles would never materialize. However, negotiations between President Kennedy and Premier Khrushchev brought an end to the conflict. Russia removed the missiles, and the USA removed its reinforced military status and equipment from the island. To ensure the commitments to remove the weapons back to a Russian ship, we spent several more weeks off shore preparing to take whatever action was called for should a missile threat rise again. After several months onboard the ship, we sailed back to California and Camp Pendleton.

Sleeping Bag and Rattle Snake Canyon

Shortly after returning to Camp Margarita, we continued our training programs, which included taking part in field maneuvers. During one such event, we made camp in Rattle Snake Canyon. This exercise included spending the night in our sleeping bags – not an inviting location to spend any time much less in a sleeping bag.

One evening, a group of us were standing around "telling war stories" when a Marine who had spent a number of years stationed at Pendleton told us about an incident that happened in Rattle Snake Canyon a few years earlier. They were camped in about the same location where we were now standing. As night set in, the troops had completed their training exercise for the day and retired to their sleeping bags for a well-deserved rest. One of the Marines crawled into his sleeping bag and fell asleep almost immediately. The night air was comfortable and the noise level that filled the daytime activities slowly disappeared, leaving the troops in a quite atmosphere. Appreciating the comfortable weather conditions, he unzipped the sleeping bag about half way down closed his eyes and fell sound asleep.

The next morning the troops were reacting to commands to get up, eat breakfast, and continue field exercises. This Marine did not move a muscle, an uncommon occurrence for a Marine on maneuvers. When his sergeant came over to offer him expert advice on motivation, he saw the tail of a rattle snake resting on the Marine's chest. The Marine looked at the sergeant, terrified, and with his free arm and hand he pointed to the snake's tail resting on his chest. The sergeant knew the worst thing he could do now was start moving.

The sergeant said, "Don't move a muscle. I will get you out of there. Remember, don't move." We are all aware one bite from a rattle snake, without an immediate anti-venom shot, could kill a person. The sergeant hurried to the commanding officer and told him about the problem and the need for immediate action. A call was made to the hospital asking for anti-venom medication. Within minutes, they could hear the noise of a helicopter bringing medical personnel and medicine to their site. As soon as it arrived, a medical team stepped out of the aircraft, rushed to the site of the Marine, and found him lying down, eyes wide open, and his body stiff as a board, truly frightened, waiting for their assistance.

The company commander and medical team reviewed the situation and decided, given the location of the snake, to remove it by force would be too dangerous. So the decision they reached was to do nothing and allow the snake to come out of the bag on its own. The sergeant returned to the Marine and told him the decision was not to take out the snake but to wait until it decided to move out on its own and return to its home in the rocks surrounding the encampment. The Marine lying there, petrified with fear, found this decision to be ill advised. Believing this newly discover visitor had plenty of sleep, he was convinced it should be removed now by force if necessary.

A look at the Marine's eyes told everyone that waiting for the snake to split company was probably not in the cards. Sweat was pouring down his face as heat from the sun coupled with his raging fear. The decision makers also knew waiting was impossible. Finally, the Marine had to do something, and waiting was not it. Everyone watched as he grabbed the snake's tail and started to yank it out of the sleeping bag. But a further problem developed when the snake was too large and too far into the bag to pull it out with one yank. He reached further down the body of the snake, grabbed it again and this time pulled it clear of the sleeping bag. As the snake hit the ground, a .45 caliber round blew its head off. However, the snake did not come out clean. During the exit, it managed to inflict several bites on his leg and side. Emergency personnel on standby administered the anti-venom shots. He was rushed to the helicopter and flown to the base hospital. His recovery took a long time.

This conversation took place just before we prepared our sleeping bags for the night. I left the group with the story of this Marine on my mind, went to my sleeping bag, opened it, shook it violently several times, crawled in, and zipped the bag shut, from top to bottom, completely covering myself, including my head. I resolved no unwelcomed visitors were going to join me for the night. At this point, I gave no thought about the hot temperature that impacted our efforts all day. However, after the first twenty minutes, I felt like a roasted turkey and unzipped the bag. The options I had left were to roast to death in the sleeping bag or take my chances with the possibility some rattlesnake or tarantula would join me for the night. After a short prayer reminding God there are more noble ways to die and I would appreciate a good night's sleep, I closed my eyes and fell sound asleep. The next morning I woke up, carefully felt around my sleeping bag, and finding it free of unwanted creatures, offered a prayer of thanks. We were taught to roll up the sleeping bag tightly before storing it, as open sleeping bags are wonderful resting areas for snakes, spiders and heaven knows what other monsters would find it an excellent resting place. We completed the operation and returned to camp. I left the area sincerely convinced I would never volunteer for duty in a snake-infested area if I could avoid it.

Benedictine Monastery

Oceanside, California, had the good fortune to have The Prince of Peace Benedictine Monastery just outside the city. Located upon a mesa, it overlooked the San Luis Rey River valley and the Pacific Ocean. The monastery took the appearance of a beacon welcoming anyone looking for a quiet day where they could relax and reflect on God and the spiritual life. The climate in Oceanside was always comfortable and the ocean breeze managed to cool down heat to comfortable levels. The location made the complex visible for miles. This monastery was founded in 1958 and, within a few years, it had a fully functioning operation. All facility upkeep was performed by the monks. They did the cooking, cleaning, laundry and all other tasks and required maintenance. Living a Benedictine life meant sharing all the domestic chores characteristic of a household. Being with them for even a short time made us aware the monks considered this their home. Everyone was welcome, made to feel at home and invited to share lunch during their visit. For someone with no culinary skills and who had to cook his own meals, a visit to the Prince of Peace Abbey had very special rewards. It became a favorite stopping off place whenever I had free time to visit.

At times I would take some of the Marines stationed at Pendleton to visit the monks and have an opportunity to see monastic life and determine if they might find it interesting enough to look into it further. Vocations to the priesthood and monastic life could be found attractive to Marines determining what career they may choose at the conclusion of their enlistment could find the Benedictines an interesting way of life. I don't know if any of the Marines I brought to the monastery seriously considered entering the Benedictine order but I do remember how much they enjoyed the time we spent there sharing the Benedictine hospitality. Some years later, I had the opportunity to meet the abbot again at the Benedictine Abbey in Canton, Louisiana where he was again managing an abbey with all the courtesies characteristic of his life.

First 20 mile hike Camp Margarita, Pendleton, CA

Marine battalion prepare for overseas assignment

Honor Guard for Armed Forces Day

Reflecting on pending action during Cuban Crisis. 1962

Field Mass offered in So Korean

Visiting Orphanage

Touring Okinawa and giving candy to children

General Nickerson welcoming Bishop Furlong

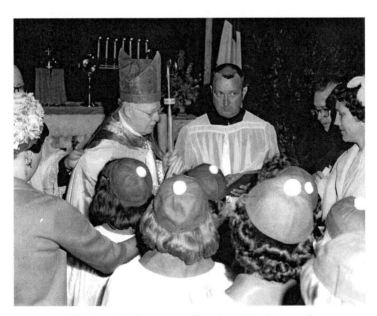

Bishop Furlong confirming Marine and
Army children – Barstow, CA

Exterior of chapel at Camp Mctureous Butler, Okinawa

Interior of the Okinawa chapel

Chapter 11
Orders to Okinawa, Japan (3rd Service Battalion)

S hortly after we returned to Camp Margarita, our outfit received orders to move overseas to Okinawa, Japan. There were a number of actions I had to take prior to leaving Camp Pendleton for the Far East. It was necessary for me to sell my car. It had a lot of years and miles on it and, by the time I returned from Okinawa, I would have to pay someone to take it. I had very few personal items, so I packed some of them to take with me to Okinawa and the rest I sent to Wausau, Wisconsin.

I had very little knowledge of Okinawa, so I made an effort to read about the island and the part it played during WWII. The fact that became so prominent was the almost unbelievable loss of human life on both sides of the conflict. I became anxious to visit some of the locations where the fighting was most furious. This would prove to be difficult as every foot of the island experienced the horror of that war. However, we had enough time in Camp Pendleton to make all the arrangements needed prior to moving to the island. The move took place during the Christmas and New Year Holidays. Fortunately we spent Christmas at Pendleton allowing the troops to spend this holiday celebrating Christmas at home with their families. Shortly after that, we sailed for Okinawa with a stopover in Hawaii where we spent New Year's Eve.

Spending the Christmas Holiday at home with their families made leaving for the Okinawa tour a little easier to accept. However, leaving the USA and their families for a tour anywhere was always difficult for families especially those with children who took the absence of their dads as hardship. Although they knew their dads had to leave them to serve at stations far from home, the separation always left them with a feeling of emptiness. Wives became both father and mother during the absence of their husbands. Managing family affairs without his input was difficult for most wives but was almost always carried out with excellence. When problems with the children or meeting unexpected expenses, health problems etc. arose, they demanded all the strength she could muster to keep normality in the daily lives of the children. Somehow, with God's help, they managed to do so.

Although leaving their families, girlfriends, and favorite sports, like golf, was difficult, most troops were ready for a change and the Far East was an intriguing place to spend their overseas tour.

On Sunday, we sailed out of Long Beach, California. As we left, the weather was excellent. Our battalion boarded the ship on a Sunday morning. I was not able to join the first units to leave the base because I had masses to offer at Camp Margarita. As soon as I had finished the masses, a Marine drove me to Long Beach where I joined the troops. Like the rest, I carried a field pack on my back as I walked to the ship. The field pack was perfectly squared away. The work of a great clerk. I boarded the ship, found my quarters, unpacked and joined the troops on the main deck. It appeared I was one of the last to board the ship. We set sail for Okinawa shortly after I arrived. Having never been to the Far East, I was anxious to get underway and excited about the opportunity to experience a way of life in a culture so different from our own. Sailing the Pacific found us moving through calm waters and comfortable weather. It proved to be a relaxing time when we would stand on the deck, watching long smooth waves push up against the side of the ship's bow, so unlike the Atlantic where the waves were always a bit rougher. The sea was calm and, as often happens on sailing trips, dolphins would appear, showing off their swimming skills by staying with the ship and riding the wash from the ship's bow. We spent considerable time talking about the Marines, the Service, and the pride of being a Marine, serving in the 5th Marines and sharing in the recognition it had earned in preceding combat situations. Occasionally, someone would become seasick, hurry to the side of the ship and empty his stomach into the ocean and on the side of the ship. At times, those who watched this action would suddenly become seasick themselves and do the same thing.

Mass was offered every day at 4 pm. This time frame was convenient for ship programs including evening meals. The period just before the Mass was used by the Colonel to give classes on Japanese, the native language of the Okinawans. After Mass, I would return to my quarters, do some reading and enjoy a late afternoon nap.

Our movement overseas allowed us some special advantages. We spent Christmas at Camp Pendleton and, on our way to Okinawa, we were scheduled to spend New Year's Eve in Honolulu, Hawaii, a beautiful island with perfect weather, great swimming and ski boarding, restaurants and shopping. Countless bars and clubs were available well into the night. When the ship docked, hundreds of Marines and Sailors disembarked moving rapidly into the city. It proved to be a great boon to our personnel and a major source of income for the businesses operating in the city.

Several of us disembarked and rented rooms at the Royal Hawaiian. There were no plans to spend a lot of time there but a room was important to store things we might buy and catch a few winks before returning to the ship.

One of our pilots knew an actress from the TV series Hawaii Five-O. He called her asking her to join us at this club. She accepted his invitation and had dinner with us. I forgot what I ordered for dinner but I do remember cleaning my plate. Eventually, everyone at our table got up and danced, except me. When they left the table to dance, I saw one of the "Airedales" pilots giving instructions to the waiter apparently giving orders about a drink. I was suspicious the discussion was about a drink for me, knowing it would prove to be a "witch's brew. Shortly after receiving his instructions, the waiter returned to the bar, picked up this special drink brought it to my table saying it was from a friend. I thanked him and tasted it and recognized this was no soft drink. It more closely resembled a powder keg and, if I drank it, I knew it would put me in a world I did not want to enter. So I signaled the same waiter. When he came to my table I told him the drink was too strong for me and to take back the drink and bring me a glass of Johnnie Walker Scotch. It would have been about the same color as the drink they ordered for me. He did as I requested and I sipped at it knowing that when they returned to the table the group would be watching to see me crash. We had a great conversation about the Island, the ship Arizona and about the wonderful experience people had riding the waves for which Hawaii was famous. After a half hour or so, they were sure they would see my head hit the table. I sipped at the scotch and participated in the table conversation. Finally, I emptied my glass, thanked them for the drink and excused myself saying it was late and I felt like it was time to get some sleep. I believe they thought I had a cast iron stomach but no one mentioned it. We stayed at the Royal Hawaiian where the accommodations were excellent for the few hours of sleep we were to get before returning to our ship. I woke up about 7:00 am dressed and looked out the window. There were a number of Marines and ship's crew lying on the lawn of the hotel still sound asleep. The temperature on the island was perfect for any kind of activity including sleeping in the open air.

When we first arrived at the Royal Hawaiian, I witnessed an act of courtesy that demonstrated a great respect for those involved. A group of formally dressed Japanese men and women were standing across from the registration counter, watching the entrance, waiting for someone to arrive. After a few minutes, another group of formally dressed Japanese entered the hotel. When all were in the lobby both groups bowed to each other with warm smiles expressing the happiness they felt toward each other. Each group walked about ten feet further into the lobby. They stopped and bowed to each other again. As the two groups came together, they stopped once more to bow to each other and then exchanged greetings. It was a sophisticated greeting ritual demonstrating their mutual respect.

The next day, several of us visited Battle Ship Arizona. The information leaflet we received discussed December 7, 1941, when Japanese aircraft bombed the Battle Ship Arizona, killing 1,177 sailors and Marines. It further stated that there are still 1,102 Sailors and Marines entombed in the ship. Following the sinking of the USS Arizona, they could hear the crew pounding on the sides of the ship for days hoping someone would hear them and take action to save them. Out of a crew of 1,511 crew members, only 334 survived. The USS Arizona Memorial lies over the ship stretching from the ship's starboard to port side. It was an extraordinary experience to be in the memorial, aware that beneath us nearly the entire ship's crew lies entombed since 1941. An interesting fact is that it was Elvis Presley who motivated a drive to construct the memorial building resting over the Arizona. He had a great respect for the men who died there and were still entombed in this ship.

Chapter 12
Life on Okinawa

We returned to the ship, continuing our trip to Okinawa, an island made famous by our struggle against Japanese soldiers trying to hold the island knowing this was the last stand they had to prevent an invasion of their homeland. Okinawa is an island off the coast of Japan. Its strategic importance to an invasion of Japan made the capture of the island a major target for the US and, for the forces of Japan, a piece of property they could not afford to lose. In taking this island, both the US Armed Forces and those of Japan suffered enormous loss of life. The struggle had great importance for both forces. For the Japanese, remaining in control of the island was vital to the course of the war. It was necessary for the Japanese to prevent it from becoming the base for the US invasion of the Japanese homeland. For the US, it meant we would be in relatively close range to Japan to carry out attacks by aircraft and as a perfect staging area for embarking our forces for an assault on Japan. The struggle was intense for both sides. The Japanese had to hold the island and we had to take it from them. The expenditures of lives and supplies were enormous as the struggle for control of the island filled the island with bodies of both Japanese and American forces. The battle for Okinawa was the largest amphibious assault in the Pacific during WW II. The Japanese combat Force designed a strategy that would allow American troops to land on the beaches with little or no resistance. But, as soon as they started inland, they would attack them from every direction. The island had countless caves, and land formations forming shelters from which they launched surprise attacks and returned to reload for the next encounter. Marines were aware of their strategy and met the challenge realistically, taking the island foot by foot. The number of troops and civilians killed taking this small island is beyond belief. The Japanese lost 107,000 soldiers. Simultaneously, tens of thousands of local civilians were killed or wounded. Our forces lost 12,373 troops during this battle, 7,373 died on the land and 5,000 were killed at sea. As we prepared to invade the Japanese homeland. we expected to lose one million American combat troops on the Japan mainland. It is obvious why a decision was made to use the atom bombs on Nagasaki and Hiroshima, Japan. Although many Japanese died in the bombing of Japan, that number would pale by comparison to the losses we and the Japanese would both experience in an invasion of Japan's homeland.

As our ship pulled up to a dock at the port city of Naha, in the south east end of Okinawa, several of us stood on the deck watching our troops disembark. While we were standing there, I became aware of a strong acid aroma permeating the air. It was strong enough to encourage asking someone what caused this smell. Several of the officers who had served in Okinawa previously said it was caused by people using the ditches alongside the roads as urinals. This is no longer the case. But, when we arrived on the island, appropriate plumbing for use by all the citizens was not available. Amazing, but after a short period of time, I was no longer conscious of this odor. In fact, I forgot all about it until I started to write this book.

We began to disembark our troop and supplies. At the same time, another US ship was being loaded with Marines and supplies for their trip back to the US. As soon as our ship was secure, we began unloading equipment, supplies and Marine personnel. Upon disembarking, a Marine envoy met me and told me my orders were changed and I was to report to Camp McTurus Butler, a Marine Supply Depot. For an island 67 miles long and 2 to 17 miles wide, it was home to thousands of Navy, Marine, Coast Guard, Army and Air Force personnel. Even though the American presence was visible throughout the island, native Okinawans dominated nearly every inch of the island. This included their presence on American properties working in stores, clubs and recreation centers. Their presence everywhere was a constant reminder we were not at home in the USA.

When I reached the base, I was assigned to officer's quarters, a long wood structure housing about twenty officers. My room was about twenty feet long and fifteen feet wide, adequate for my needs, i.e. the contents of two suitcases. It had a bed and closets. The bathing and shaving facilities were located in the middle of the hallway equally accessible to all the troops. I entered my room and put away my belongings then I visited my neighbors Jack Gillen and Joe Poquette who shared the adjacent room. We served together for months and became lifelong friends. Eventually, we went to my room and as I entered I saw a salamander crawling on the wall just over my bed. I said, "Good Lord, what the hell is that thing doing in my room? I had better kill it." I did not need a green creature crawling around my room, especially at night. They both said, almost together, "don't kill it. The salamander eats the flies and other vermin found in the area. They are really a friendly creature." For the first few nights I felt uneasy watching it move around the walls but, eventually, I almost forgot they were even there.

The officer's club was at the top of a hill on our base with a path leading down to our building. The location and services were outstanding. In the evenings, I would spend time at the club having a drink, listening to music, playing pool and spending time talking with the ladies tending the bar and the other patrons. We were all aware we had a pack of wild dogs on the base but were never really concerned, mostly because we almost never saw them. When they were seen, it was generally at night. However, they were dangerous because they could do some real damage to our personnel should they attack us. One evening, one of the officers from our building left the club and started down the path to his quarters. Half way down he saw a bunch of these wild dogs running at him. He ran as fast as he could and barely got into the building before they reached him. Obviously, the problem had become serious and the base commander sent a hunting party to eradicate all of the dogs. Shortly thereafter, we heard gun shots and packs of wild dogs no longer inhabited our area.

Habu and the Mongoose

A major concern was the presence of the habu snake found throughout the Island. It posed a problem to everyone on Okinawa. This snake's venomous bite could result in serious physical harm or death to its victim. The habu was a large snake with a length of about 4 to 5 feet. It had a large head and was so quick at making a strike it could do so in the blink of an eye. They were found throughout the island generally in vegetation, on rocky surfaces, in caves and at times in people's homes where it searched for rats and other vermin. Additionally, there were mongooses who were bitter enemies of the habu. The mongoose had a long face, gradually tapering down to its mouth. Its body weighed from two to nine pounds with short legs and a long fur covered body. This animal was so fast it could strike before the habu could react. When this combat took place, it was a fight to the death. For those of us who watched the "Meeker" on Sunday afternoon television would recognize the general appearance of what the mongoose would look like. On maneuvers in the jungles of Okinawa, troops were always aware they could come in contact with a habu. One of the troops, while crawling on the ground through some vegetation, grabbed a piece of barbed wire. Thinking he had just been bit by a habu, he jumped up and yelled for a medic. A quick review of the situation revealed the real problem to the relief of everyone in the area.

I had an opportunity to attend a habu vs. mongoose fight in a shack a good ways from our camp. The stage was a wood floor with a cage containing a mongoose. On the deck was a habu, its head up waiting for something to happen. Around the stage were a few dozen Okinawan men betting on the outcome of this conflict. Most were smiling while some appeared to be extremely serious as if their bet used their homes as collateral. The fight started, when the cage was opened and the mongoose was dropped onto the stage a few feet away from the habu. The reaction of the mongoose to the habu was immediate. His head turned to look at the habu and in seconds he leaped toward the habu's neck but missed because the habu, equally alert and competent, pulled back its head, causing the mongoose to miss its target. The mongoose made a swift move away from the habu and crouched into a position for another attack. He hesitated a few seconds as if contemplating his next move. He lunged again biting the habu's body while constantly watching the head of the habu as it got into position to lunge at the mongoose. The snake attacked the mongoose with one of its lighting fast strikes. It took place so fast I could not see if it had been successful. By this time the mongoose had blood splattered around its mouth and cheeks from the bites it had taken on the habu's body. Both contestants began maneuvering for an advantageous position. It was obvious this was a struggle to the death. Finally, the habu made another strike at the mongoose and, as it tried to return to its defensive position, the mongoose made another lunge at the snake's throat, got hold of it and shook it while biting through the habu's neck. The mongoose kept biting and shaking the habu until it believed the snake was dead. Even after the snake was killed, its coils kept moving, curling up, appearing to be still alive. However, the mongoose was sure he won the battle, even though the blood stains made it seem as if he had taken a few hits as well. The person responsible for the mongoose moved it back into its cage and locked it. Onlookers began to pay off their bets, discussing how long they thought the mongoose would live, knowing it had been bitten by the snake at least two times. I am sure this would now be considered cruelty to animals, which it probably was. However, as the action took place, everyone was absorbed in watching the event. I made my way out of the building, caught a cab and returned to my base.

The island still had scars from the WWII conflict. High cliffs used by the natives to commit suicide rather than surrender to advancing American troops gave us a sense of the fear that terrorized the natives. In preparation for the invasion by the US Forces, Japanese soldiers and Okinawan citizens moved into caves, with intermingled tunnels, communications systems and numerous defensive bunkers to resist our forces. Japan's plan called for allowing our troops to land on the island with little or no resistance. Then destroy them as they moved inland. Native Okinawans believed the Americans were determined to destroy them along with the Japanese. However, they eventually changed their minds when the Americans fixed their wounds, gave them shelter and food and offered them the courtesies of friends.

The landing of our troops on Okinawa was the largest amphibious assault in the Pacific War. The battle for Okinawa was fought by four Divisions of the US Army and Two Marine Corps Divisions. The battles lasted eighty days. When the battles were under control, preparation began for the invasion of Japan. Although not directly related to an Okinawan experience, the raid of Lt. Col. James Doolittle was a major source of celebration in the U.S. and for our troops in the Pacific. In April 1942, Lt. Col. Doolittle, flying B-25 aircraft, launched a raid on the Japanese homeland from the decks of the aircraft carrier *Hornet*. Although the raid did little to halt the Japanese war production, it was a diversion that boosted American and allied morale. Although it had limited goals, it did serve to demonstrate to Japanese leadership they were vulnerable to air attacks. This was followed by numerous air attacks with devastating results by B-29 Aircraft. Then the stratofortress bombers were introduced into the bombing of Japan. These Aircraft flew at such heights the Japanese anti-aircraft weapons could not reach them. They brought severe damage to Japan, its industries and population. It is estimated the raids killed between 241,000 and 900,000 people. The aircraft carrier USS *Shangri-La* (CVA-38) played a major role in defeating the Japanese through the constant air raids on territories occupied by Japan. It received the nickname The Tokyo Express. Years later I served on the *Shang* for two years - a part of which included a Mediterranean Cruise; a great ship with a great crew.

Exploding two atomic bombs on the major Japanese cities Hiroshima and Nagasaki led to the end of the War in the Pacific. An interesting observation concerns a Catholic priest who was teaching at a Japanese University in Hiroshima at the time of the explosion. Although the university was miles away from the explosions, he had his back to the window in the classroom when the bomb exploded. In a talk he gave upon his return to the US, he said glass from the windows behind him ripped into his back causing considerable harm.

Native Okinawans experienced the force of this invasion. I was told of a rumor spread among native Okinawans and Japanese soldiers. "To be accepted into the Marine Corps they had to kill their mother or father." This rumor caused a real fear of the invading Marines. Expecting abuse by our troop, women and children jumped off cliffs to commit suicide. Others moved into the dozens of caves found on the island. Many of the caves were also inhabited by Japanese soldiers and used for surprise attacks on our forces. Not knowing who may be hiding in them, our troops called into the caves telling them to come out and surrender. Often, the calls went unanswered. Not knowing if Japanese soldiers or civilians were hidden in them, a flame thrower was used to eliminate anyone finding refuge in the caves. Native

Okinawans who did surrender to our troops discovered they were treated kindly, fed, clothed and given necessary medical attention - as much as could be done under the combat conditions. The benign manner in which native Okinawans were treated by our Marines and army personnel spread slowly. However, countless numbers of Okinawans remained unaware our assault was tempered with a sense of humanity for the non-combatants.

The Japanese were aware this island was the last defense against an invasion of mainland Japan. The fighting was fierce. The sheer numbers of Allied ships and armored vehicles that assaulted the island was enormous. Simultaneously, tens of thousands of local civilians were killed, wounded, or committed suicide. The history of this Island and the vital role it played in WWII continues to this day. Remnants of this struggle can be found in a visit to almost any part of the Island.

At the time we were stationed on the island, older Okinawan generations still had memories of WWII. But the rest of the population became engaged in the commerce that was now flourishing throughout the island. Cities were developing, roads built, and hundreds of positions with the military were filled by natives with a huge number who spoke English (although with a definite Okinawan accent). Sanitary conditions in many parts of the island remained as they were a hundred years earlier with ditches serving as urinals. Overall, the natives adjusted to our presence and were comfortable dealing with American troops.

The island golf course received considerable use. At times it would rain during the game but the heat from the sun was strong enough to dry our clothes quickly, hardly delaying the game. I remember an occasion when Col. Reese was just leaving for the golf course when I commented he was wearing proper gear for the game. Being a less than average golfer I appreciated his response. "You have to look like a great golfer when you walk on to the course, even if you're a duffer."

Okinawan citizens were employed by all the bases. Some of them were employed as waitresses, some cleaned officer quarters and many worked as waiters in base cafeterias and did other jobs at each station. An interesting practice was the promotion system. Promotions were accelerated by the person's ability to learn and use the English language. It proved to be an excellent motivator. The more fluent their English became, the more they were eligible for salary increases.

The brig maintained at McTurus Butler is a place of internment for Marines and sailors who "got crossways" with the law. A book written by Madison Powell about this brig tells a story of intrigue, and destructive politics making this facility a trip to hell. How true this was I don't know. But, years later, as the base chaplain, I found it managed by competent, highly- trained security personnel with close oversight of prisoner activities, including their health needs. After all it was a prison: a place of internment for violating laws. Prisoners were denied many of the privileges available to the Marines and Naval personnel stationed on this island. Discipline was fair but stern enough to encourage prisoners to change behavior patterns that messed up their lives. Sometimes, "bad things happen to good people" is a principle occasionally verified in visits to a brig. Regardless, this statement does not negate the position that bringing their religious beliefs into everyday life is a great deterrent to behavior that will ultimately result in brig time. I don't recall ever meeting prisoners who brought the practice of their religion into their daily lives.

The island had numerous restaurants and night clubs owned and managed by Okinawan natives. As a safety measure, the restaurants and night clubs were inspected and formally approved for use by the military. Appropriate steps were taken to ensure an acceptable standard of cleanliness and safety of food and drinks served to military personnel. Other restaurants preferred to serve Okinawans mainly catering to the island's native population. They were not subject to military inspections because they preferred to serve natives. Military personnel were prohibited from using their services. Their clientele followed the oriental tradition of taking off their shoes at the entrance of the facility and eating their meals sitting on a rugged floor at a table a foot or so off the floor; unusual but comfortable. Military police would check out restaurants by looking for shoe sizes and design. It was rather easy to determine if Americans were eating there by the size and style of the shoes at the entrance to the restaurant. Military authorities checked the approved restaurants and clubs to ensure the facilities' standards of cleanliness and safety of food preparations were honored. When a facility was found acceptable, an "A" sign was posted on the facility in an easily observed location. The "A" sign was placed outside the building so troops could know the place met acceptable standards. Several Japanese restaurants did not cater to military clientele so there was no "A" sign attached to their entrances.

Some members of the Armed Forces wished to enjoy the Japanese customs of dining using chop sticks, sitting on a rugged floor and eating at a table a foot off the floor. To avoid unwanted attention by the MPs, we would take our shoes off and carry them to their dining rooms. Those of us who had motor scooters with a military license plate would back the scooter up to the wall of the building hiding the license plate so it would not be recognized by the MPs. The Okinawans also drove scooters and parked their vehicles in the same place and manner.

One characteristic found in the native restaurants was their manner of taking orders for their meals. They always exhibited respect for the person served by offering traditional Japanese courtesies to their customers. They would kneel next to the person and write down the order. In most cases, we had no knowledge of the language. But, knowing the food to be always great, we could point to a name and hope for the best. However, most of the time eating off base meant going to another base for dinner. Kadena Air Force base proved to be the favored officer's club on the Island.

Catholic chaplains from all the services gathered at the Air Force Officer's Club every Sunday night for dinner together. Generally, we numbered around a dozen chaplains and found this time an important occasion as it often proved to be the only time we were able to be together and discuss events taking place back in the States and on our island bases. The meals were excellent and the service was outstanding. One feature of the club remembered by those of us stationed on the island was the waitress who served our table. Every Sunday, she managed the job alone. She was absolutely beautiful, always serious and meticulous in ensuring that each order was taken accurately and served properly. She never wrote a note on any of our orders. She had a prodigious memory. One Sunday evening, we had about twelve or so priests eating dinner together. We all knew she had an extraordinary memory. So, we decided to test her memory. Each of us ordered a different drink, believing there was no way she could keep all these orders separate and serve each drink to the person making the order. She never used paper and pen. She took each order by memory which naturally made us assume she would make at least a few mistakes with orders for twelve people. We had difficulty coming up with different drinks she would have to remember. About fifteen minutes after she took the orders, she returned and placed each of our orders before us without making a single mistake. It was absolutely amazing. There were many accomplished Okinawans with enviable skills. But she will be remembered by all of us as the best of the best.

There was a heavily trafficked enlisted club located in Naha City on the south end of the island. It had a reputation of featuring a native singer, who was also the club owner's daughter. This girl specialized in singing American songs. She had memorized the songs in English and delivered them with all the finesse of an accomplished performer. She could mesmerize the troops who all found her performances to be a touch of home. Although she could put appropriate emotion into each song, we were told she did not understand the lyrics in most of the songs. It made no difference to her audience who was there to enjoy her performance and not to evaluate her grasp of the English language.

Taipei, Taiwan

Catholic chaplains went on a retreat once a year to review and evaluate our lives over the past year and to make plans to improve over the upcoming year. This has been a common practice for chaplains, for decades. Being overseas is not an exception. This time I went to Taipei, Taiwan, to join Spike O'Donnell and other chaplains who were fulfilling this same task. Spike and I became good friends. When serving on the carrier we received repairs at the Norfolk Naval Station where he was stationed. I visited him as often as my time allowed. Fortunately, during this trip I was able to visit a Jesuit mission on the island. They had established, employed and trained native Taiwanese in making furniture and other wood products. Their works were extraordinary for quality and appearance. The chapel on

McTurus Butler did not have a crucifix appropriate for use when Mass was offered. The store had a large selection, allowing me to make a selection appropriate for the size and décor of the altar in the base chapel.

The carpentry skills of the craftsmen working at the mission were extraordinary. The shop had numerous examples of beautifully designed furniture, desks and other items appropriate for any home. One item caught my eye. It was a cabinet designed to be a music station to hold musical equipment, records, and recording equipment. Other features made it a most useful and attractive piece of furniture. I bought it and had it shipped to Okinawa for further transfer to the USA upon my transfer back to the States. When my transfer arrived, I returned via aircraft and was unable to take the cabinet with me. So, Joe Poquette arranged to ship it when he returned to the States; a really great favor.

There were the O'Brien identical twin brothers, Brian and Paul from Escanaba, Michigan a city in the Diocese of Marquette, Michigan, who were ordained priests of the Maryknoll missionaries. They were stationed at a Maryknoll mission in Taiwan. When they had some time off, they flew to Okinawa for a visit with their fellow "Michigander." They do great work and what absolutely amazed me was their ability to speak Chinese fluently. The Mandarin language, is tonal, having four levels to distinguish words that otherwise would sound the same. I believe they have now returned to the States. I have never been able to tell them apart.

Following the retreat, we all went to a local golf club to play eighteen holes before returning to our duty stations on Taiwan and Okinawa. We each had a native caddy. My caddy was a genius. Playing golf like a guerrilla, I sliced my ball on a number of occasions and thought it entered the rough. As we walked to the brushes where I thought the ball had entered, I would see him diligently looking for the ball. Then he would glance back to the fairway raise his hand, and point to the ball a foot or so into the fairway. On one such occasion, I saw him moving in the brushes and looking down intensely for my ball. When he found it, I saw him catch the ball between his toes, walk out of the brush still aggressively looking for the ball and then let it down on the fairway a few feet from the rough then call me, pointing at its new location. I ended up with a decent score and gave him a generous tip. His service was well worth the cost. The next day, I flew back to Okinawa and resumed my post. Shortly after returning to the island, I was promoted to lieutenant. I borrowed a Marine officer's dress uniform as proper attire when the base commander pinned on my bars.

Chapter 13
Landing in Korea and Two Trips
to an Orphanage

S ince WWII, the US has had a military presence on Okinawa: both as a staging area in the event of conflict in the Far East, and as a training ground where all branches of our military services maintain operations. The Marines 3rd Division had several infantry camps on Okinawa, all of which were part of the huge Marine presence on the island. We experienced the practicality of the Okinawan location when the tenth anniversary of the Korean War armistice arose. Possible trouble from North Korea was anticipated and operations to defend the South were made. Being on Okinawa, we were logistically located to move our troops to Korea within a reasonable time frame. Our troops were combat ready. It was necessary for us to move to South Korea as a bulwark against North Korea in the event the North decided to invade the South again. Troops stationed in Okinawa were assigned the task of being the first bulwark against an invasion.

An armistice was signed in Panmunjom on July 27, 1953, resolving the Korean War. Ten years later, the economic status of North Korea was bleak. We understood the leadership was looking for some reason to take the minds of their citizens off their starvation diets and scarce employment opportunities by staging another invasion into South Korea, a much more developed and prosperous economy. Allies had troops in South Korea but not in sufficient numbers to withstand a full scale invasion. The Demilitarized Zone (DMZ) developed along the 38th parallel separated the two Koreas. The zone was 160 miles long and about 2 ½ miles wide. It is the most heavily militarized border in the world to this day. There have been numerous incursions by the North into the South resulting in the deaths of hundreds of soldiers on both side of the DMZ. Numerous, often clandestine, attacks were made on the South in efforts to enflame the South to respond militarily, but without success. One of the North's better known programs was the development of tunnels of various sizes under the DMZ. Four of the tunnels were discovered ranging in size from five feet high by four feet wide, to one fully developed with electricity and stable walls allowing it to accommodate moving thousands of troops and combat equipment across the border. The possibility of an invasion called for more boots on the ground, which included moving troops from Okinawa to the DMZ.

Deploying from a U.S. Naval ship filled with Marines is always risky business. This landing on the shore of South Korea had few problems with the exception of some cold temperatures. Marines were to be deployed south of the thirty-eighth parallel, the imaginary line dividing the communist North Korea from the capitalist South Korea. A considerable amount of time was spent in Okinawa preparing for such incursions by North Korea. When the time arrived to move out, we were more than ready. We boarded ships carrying supplies, combat equipment and Naval and Marine personnel. When disembarking, the troops would climb down a rope net hanging down the side of the ship, step off the net into a landing barge. Given the rise and fall of wave actions, it was safest to step into the landing barge when the waves were at their highest level. Movement of the waves could vary from a few feet to five feet or more. At times, disembarking would result in accidents from stepping into a barge carrying all their gear when waves alongside a ship fell several feet making it an occasion for serious injury. At times, the troops would not react in concert with the movement of the waves and fall several feet to the bottom of the barge, sometimes resulting in broken ankles, arms, etc. (I don't recall any of our troops being injured while disembarking for this operation.) This phase of the trip was accomplished without difficulty. We boarded ships, sailed to the border of South Korea and disembarked in Marine fashion, climbing down nets strung over the side of the ships into landing crafts that carried us ashore. Troops, supplies and equipment were moved ashore and headquarters set up in a clearing found in a virgin forest of towering trees and thick, dark green vegetation obscuring objects a mile away.

However, unlike actual combat conditions, we were greeted by a crowd of children filled with excitement watching this mass of men and equipment move into place. We received their smiles and waves of welcome. They were dressed in tee shirts, shorts and sandals. They were shivering and had their arms pressed closely to their chests trying to generate a bit of warmth as they watched the extravaganza of us moving into our staging area. Being close to the ocean, the weather was cold and damp. The children were not the least bit afraid of us, although they kept their distance. After our tents were set up, we ate and I took the opportunity to walk around the combat operations center then turned in for the night.

The next morning, troops were moving out, setting up communication centers, supply routes and doing dozens of other activities - characteristic of preparation for combat operations. The area seemed desolate. One well maintained gravel road reached our staging area and led away from our site to a beautiful green forest and beyond. It seemed to invite someone to explore wherever it led. A Marine sergeant and I decided to take the unspoken invitation. Sarge drove our jeep around our compound and started down this newly discovered gravel road. The trip took us through heavily wooded areas with dark green leaves dense enough to conceal everything beyond them. Steep, wet inclines were characteristic of road conditions. On several occasions, we stopped at clearings to admire the beauty surrounding us. On one of these stops, a huge Marine truck came over the hill behind us; saw our parked jeep and tried to stop but was unable to do so, it slammed into the back of our jeep. Sarge saw it coming. He turned the wheels away from the ravine just in time to send us sailing down the road. I am so thankful to Sarge's quick thinking. The alternative would have found us a part of the scenery fifty feet below!

Tree formations and the mingling of bright orange and green underbrush covered the roots of the trees like blankets carefully placed to protect them from the frost and cold. Several miles further we turned a corner and unexpectedly drove into a complex of buildings which included a three story gray building that appeared to be a school or some sort of dormitory. Although the buildings were showing signs of aging, they appeared to be well maintained. A few of the buildings were obviously residences and a church. Within seconds we realized we had arrived at a huge orphanage with dozens of children running, playing games, and thoroughly occupied in their activities. We were surprised by the size of the operation and the number of children playing in the compound. One group looked like they were playing soccer while other groups watched the game or were involved in other activities.

Orphanage

We drove slowly as we entered the compound. When the children saw us they stopped what they were doing and stood motionless. They watched us as we drove slowly to a group of children surrounding a nun who was demonstrating her skill for fixing broken toys. We drove up to the nun and introduced ourselves as US Marines on maneuvers in this part of South Korea. She was taken by surprise but seemed happy to see us. She did not speak English. Her greeting *"bonjour"* confirmed she was French and her brown habit said she was a Franciscan nun.

She pointed to the rectory, motioning us to follow her. A priest from France who managed the operation, came out of the rectory to greet us. I remembered some of the French I had in high school, very little, and Father knew some English, very little. My asking intelligently for a cup of coffee in French would have been a stretch. The French priest's knowledge of English and my knowledge of French were sufficient to establish a meager form of communication. Hand signals played a part in this communication session. We did communicate sufficiently enough to grasp some understanding of who each of us were. I asked him how many children were at the orphanage and was told there were roughly one hundred. They survived with gifts from France and donations from other charitable organizations. The children looked healthy. They managed to find enough food to keep them from starving and enough clothing to lock out some of the cold air. It did not take long to realize finding enough food to feed so many children was a major responsibility. The main building was three stories tall and clean. The church and rectory seemed efficiently designed but lacking in the electronics and other office equipment characterizing institutions in the US. Father served us coffee mixed with a thick cream-like substance. The drink was excellent. Whatever the mix was, it certainly made the coffee a memorable drink. We spent an hour or so and drove back to the staging area, happy we found them and were able to manage a conversation with the orphanage staff.

It was early evening and a number of us were sitting down eating our dinner rations discussing the poverty demonstrated by the children who witnessed our arrival and how helpless we felt to alleviate some of these problems. A naval officer from the ship's crew mentioned that within the next few days they were going out to sea to discard stores of food due to reach their expiration date. This seemed like a God send. I thought: we may not be able to help everyone but I knew a place where a truck full of food would feed a lot of children. I left the camp and took a liberty boat to the ship and requested to talk with the captain. After we had talked for a few minutes I told him about the orphanage and the great number of children living there. I mentioned the information I received concerning the ship's return to sea to dump outdated supplies. Then I asked him if he would consider giving some of those supplies destined to be discarded to the orphanage. His first reaction was no. He did not think it prudent because if someone got sick on the food, the US would be held responsible. I asked him if he had a date for discarding the food and he mentioned it would be within the next few weeks. I suggested that if we could eat this food for a period of time, it would be presumed safe. So, perhaps, taking some of it to the orphanage would not be imprudent since the expiration date was some time away. It would be a considerably generous gift from the people of the USA. We discussed it for a while and he gave his okay and told me the food would be ready for pick up the next morning. The ship planned to set sail early afternoon the next day, so our pickup time had to be early the next morning. The next morning, I hurried to the Marine staging area and commandeered a huge four-ply truck and several Marines to return to the ship. The skipper had already notified the crew who was waiting for us ready to load the supplies. We packed the cartons as high as the truck could safely hold them and returned to the orphanage.

When we reached the compound, around noon, we drove to the main building and told the priest we had some food he could use to feed the children who, by now, had gathered around our truck anxiously waiting to find out what the boxes held. I told him the truck was ready to be unloaded and asked him where the proper place would be to unload the truck. He suggested a location. We drove to it and began unloading the boxes. The surprise and smiles on the faces of the staff and children spoke volumes. We quickly unloaded and stacked the cartons. I broke open a box, took a ration and broke the seal. Each of the rations contained a thick chocolate bar. I took out the chocolate bar and handed it to a little boy the priest was holding in his arms. The child was hesitant to accept it, but Father told him to take a bite. He did so and in a few seconds turned to us with a face illuminated with a huge smile. The other children looked up anxious to share such a treat. There was sufficient food to feed all hands for at least a week maybe more. As we prepared to leave we received their thanks and drove back to the beach. Their thanks were appreciated but the smile on that child's face as he tasted chocolate for the first time will always remain deeply embedded in my memory.

Visitors of the Night

One evening, night had settled in. The movement of vehicles and supplies that filled our days gave way to a quiet, comfortable evening. The sky was overcast and the increasing darkness obscured much of our outfit including the high ridges about a hundred yards or so to the north of our camp. As I returned to my area I heard voices coming from the ridges. A number of "ladies of the night" were offering their services to the troops, all of whom had been made aware that relations with them would give them painful souvenirs they could very well carry with them for the rest of their lives. Some of visitors managed to make their way into the camp proper hiding in bushes, behind equipment attempting to ply their trade. To prevent this kind of activity, Korean security was stationed around our camp. When any of the ladies were found in or close to the camp, they would be arrested, placed in a truck and taken out of the area.

On my way back to my station, I passed a very large bush in the middle of the pathway. As I walked pass it, a hand reached out of the bush and grabbed my sleeve and whispered "piece of a–. I jumped to the side, surprised any of them could get this far into our area. I answered, "I think you just grabbed the wrong sleeve." About seventy-five yards away from us, two Korean guards were standing and noticed I had stopped and was talking to someone hiding in the bush. Within a minute or so they were at my side, reaching into the bushes and yanking out two of them, one of whom appeared to fall but managed to catch her balance. Slinging them to the middle of the pathway they signaled the truck driver to pick them up. When the tuck arrived, the guards grabbed them, violently threw them onto the truck causing one of them to lose a slipper that fell at my feet. Believing this piece of clothing would probably be a serious financial loss, I picked it up, intending to throw it onto the truck. This all happened so fast, the truck began immediately to move out before I could reach it. I ran after it for a few yards and gave up, unable to get close enough to make the throw. I stopped and looked back at the Korean guards who looked puzzled, amazed someone even cared. Sometimes, I think I should have kept it as a souvenir to remember that evening.

Chapter 14
Return to the USA

W hen our assignment was completed, we returned to our base on Okinawa with some wonderful memories that would live with us for a lifetime. Several weeks later I received orders to report to the Marine Corps base in Barstow, California with an assignment as Catholic Chaplain.

One of the programs the Catholic chaplains had when they were transferred out of Okinawa was to prepare a "Mount out Box" for our replacements and, truth be told, it had very little substantive content or useful information. The main element to be turned over to the replacement was the transfer of a car. The "Mount out Box" (priced at a cost of $400) I had to pay for. It was the price all the chaplains paid for many previous years. It was my intention to sell it to my replacement, rusted parts and all. The car was a very old, but still a functioning Chevrolet, probably from the 1950s. It was black and had several unseemly rust holes that did nothing to enhance the car's appearance. I decided to do something about the rust holes found mostly around the hood and fenders. I bought some masking tape and black gloss paint to cover the holes. I covered all the rust spots with the masking tape and then painted over the hood and fenders. From a distance it appeared to be okay. My replacement would be delighted to have a car and admire the good shape the vehicle was in. Unfortunately, but with some degree of humor, two days later it rained and we watched the tape begin to shrivel up and reveal the skeletal remains he would purchase. Since this car was probably one of the only private vehicles on the island, I knew he would be delighted to have it, just as I was a year earlier.

Trip Back to Pendleton and Waitress Serving Civilians First

Our trip back to the USA began by boarding a military aircraft at Kadena Air Force Base. All the passengers were members of one or other of the Services represented on the island. Shortly after becoming airborne, our aircraft began circling the airport. Having very little knowledge of problems an aircraft could experience, I felt it was the job of the pilot to work it out. Sitting in the seat next to me was a pilot sound asleep. As if notified by some interior power, he came awake with a jolt and, turning to me, he asked what the problem was. I told him we were told the plane could not get the landing gear to go back into the body of the plane and the crew was trying to work out the problem. That seemed to ease his mind. He leaned back into his seat and again went sound asleep. That exercise lasted about fifteen minutes. When the problem was solved we continued the trip to Japan where we caught a commercial airline and joined civilian passengers, for the trip to the States. We did not have a great deal of free time in Japan to eat a meal or buy souvenirs. We weren't too concerned because we were told we would have plenty of food and drinks aboard the plane during our trip back to the USA. It was late afternoon when we arrived at the airport. Japan was our first stop on our trip back to the Continental USA with a final stop at the Marine base in Pendleton, California.

We had flown about two or three hours when the stewardess announced over the loud speaker she would now serve our meals. By this time we could have eaten the cartons the food came in. She followed this announcement by stating civilians would be served first and after they had been served, the military personnel would be served. We must have had twenty-five or more military onboard the flight and being treated like second-class citizens really ticked off every one of us on the plane. When she finished serving the civilians she started to bring dinners to military personnel. Not one of us accepted the dinner. She was begging us over the loud speaker to take a meal asking "What am I going to do with all these dinners?" We probably all felt like telling her where to stuff the dinners but we decided to make no comments. When the plane landed in Alaska, we went to the coin machines and consumed almost all the food in the lobby coin machines. After several hours, we boarded a flight to Los Angeles. After a stopover at Pendleton, I took a week of leave to spend with my parents and family in Wausau, Wisconsin. Following the leave I reported to the Marine base at Barstow, California.

Chapter 15
Barstow Duty and Vegas Trip

When I arrived at Barstow, I reported to the base commander and senior chaplain, my supervisor, a gentleman and a pleasure to work with. In so many ways he was an extraordinary person and supervisor. I wanted to live off base and I requested authority to do. Evan Greco, the Catholic chaplain I followed at the base, was able to spend a week or so before he had to report to his new assignment. He went with me to a real estate agent in town looking for a house for sale. We were told that a contractor in Barstow had just completed a home he had built for his family. They had not yet moved into the home; the realtor thought he would sell it as his family was comfortable in their present home. We met with the contractor at the house in question. It had three bedrooms; two bathrooms, a large kitchen and a fenced in backyard. He agreed to sell it to me and asked the realtor to handle the sale. The purchase price for the house was $14,000. Before buying this house, my biggest purchase was a car to be paid for over a period of years. So I had no idea of the processes one has to go through to buy a house. I told the salesman I liked the house and would be interested in buying it. During the discussion the subject of a $500 down payment arose. I did not have that much money available in my pocket or in my checking account. I thanked him for his efforts and we made our way back to the base. On our way back we discussed moving onto Officers quarters on base. Evan asked how much money I had. I had $40. He said "you might just as well be broke." He made a suggestion we go to Las Vegas and try to win the $500. I agreed and we left for Vegas the same afternoon. When we arrived in Vegas, I filled the car with gas to make sure we had enough fuel to return to base in the event I went broke. We selected the Tropicana hotel, parked the car and went immediately to the craps table. We agreed we would leave Vegas no later than 6:00 am the next morning regardless of any success or loss.

The dealers, several of whom were former Marines, were aware we were Marines and gave us some help in playing the odds. We won and lost throughout the night. At 6:00 am I was down to $2 and Evan was at the same level. We drove away from the club with the intention of stopping at a restaurant outside Vegas for a $2 breakfast. It was Monday morning when we arrived; the place was closed for the day. So, after a short discussion, we decided to put the remainder of our cash to good use. We decided to return to the Tropicana and spend the $2 on a worthy cause – money to buy the house in Barstow. We went back to the Tropicana laid down the $2 on the craps table, and watched a player roll the dice. I won!!! I kept winning until I had the $500 down payment. We knew WHO to thank for this win. The next day, we went to the real estate agent and gave him the $500. He knew we found the cash in Vegas. Then we proceeded to move into the house over the next few days. I had wonderful neighbors and thoroughly enjoyed living there for the next two years. John Morley, a fellow chaplain I had met during our chaplain training period in Rhode Island, had been transferred from an Alaskan base to 29 Palms, California. Arriving late one winter night, he took a room at a Barstow motel. The next morning he called me around breakfast time telling me he had been transferred to 29 Palms and where he was staying. The temperature outside was cold for us living in Barstow. So, I put on my field jacket and drove to the motel. When I arrived, all the doors to all the rooms in the motel were shut tight to keep out the cold, except one. The door was ajar and the lights were on in the room. I determined John had to be there. Cold for us would not be cold for him. When I entered, John was sitting on his bed fully dressed, comfortable in the Barstow freeze. This was a real switch from the freezing weather at his last duty station. Since 29 Palms was relatively close to Barstow, we had the opportunity to get together on occasion. When he did have a chance to visit, we would make our way to Vegas. One Sunday afternoon, I got a call from John telling me there had been a rain storm up in the mountains and he was watching boulders and other debris run down a riverbed that an hour ago was absolutely dry. He said the flow of water was running so fast he was not able to cross the river. About a half hour later, he called again telling me the water flow was now barely moving and he could cross it. I discovered that a large, wide, dry river bank could become a monster when the rains in the mountains push the water down its slopes and fill the river banks in a matter of minutes. Someone crossing it could be in serious danger if caught in it unaware of the power the river could have moving from the mountains into the streams below.

Family Life in Barstow

The Marine Corps Supply and Maintenance Base in Barstow, California proved to be a great place for family life giving me a chance to function almost like a pastor in a civilian community. Marines were home with their wives and children. It was a marvelous experience for chaplains because they could take part in the lives of the families and participate in their activities on and off the base. As with all Marine bases, enlisted housing was made available to Marine families. The apartments were adequately furnished, making the places comfortable though not extravagant. Some families would purchase items like a car, washing machine, clothing and other things to make some improvements in their standard of living and demonstrate their love for the wives. Doing this at times brought about some problems. The age of the married couples, in the lower grades, is generally in their late teens and some in their early twenties. In most cases, the Marine couples were happily married and stayed within their financial status. Other times, problems would occur. Two major factors would come into play when it came to making expenditures: One is newly married couples are barely out of high school with little or no grounding in making thought-out financial decisions. The other is the level of the income they receive in their starting grades. The salary is acceptable but for married couples it leaves very little room for extraneous spending. Human nature being what it is, wives sometimes brag to other Marine wives how much her husband loved them by showing them the gift she received. Occasionally, it would motivate other wives to encourage their husbands to buy similar things for them. When they are unable or unwilling to make monthly payments, their relations become strained by the pressure from the company from whom they made this purchase. Most couples think through the issues and make arrangements to manage the problem appropriately. In some cases very little thought is given to the impact a purchase can have when their salary level is insufficient to cover expenses they incur. In such cases, when the husband decides he cannot afford the item, his wife becomes angry and hounds him to make purchases beyond their capacity to meet the payments. Real problems follow, sometimes ending in divorce or other destructive actions. Sometimes, bad judgment creates problems that threaten or destroy the stability of the marriage. I can recall one such event in which I became involved.

Attempted Suicide

It began on a Sunday afternoon following a busy Sunday morning. I received a call from the California Highway Patrol shortly after lunch. A phone call from the police never forebodes good news especially on a military base with thousands of Marines; most of them recently graduated from high school and some with little experience in managing their freedom in a mature manner. On this particular Sunday afternoon, after offering two Masses, I had a short breakfast and a chance to sit down with a cup of hot coffee and a copy of the LA Times. The phone rang; I picked it up expecting to hear "How about a golf game?" This call was different. The caller identified himself as Sgt. Williams with the California Highway Patrol. "We have a problem," he stated. "There is a Marine standing on top of the Expressway Bridge saying he is going to jump. We encouraged him to come down and discuss his problem and told him no problem is worth committing suicide." The officer had managed to get within ten feet of the jumper but was warned not to come any closer. He heard the jumper murmuring something about his wife leaving him; she didn't love him anymore; and his life was not worth living. I asked the Sergeant "do you know the name of the Marine?" He answered "I asked the jumper for his name but he refused to answer. Someone in the crowd watching the man said "his name was "Jimmy Newman."

This brought a flurry of thoughts to my mind. I knew about the couple. They were married for about a year and were living in base housing. I knew the marriage was having problems. Neighbors talked about his wife screaming at him so loudly it was heard in other nearby trailers. I remember hearing Jim and his wife were having problems regarding their household furnishings. Other enlisted men had purchased washers and dryers, cars, made long-distance phone calls and other items which set them back financially. Generally, these problems were managed without severely disrupting their lives. Newman, however, had a rather unusual but very real problem. The word was his wife was a former LA prostitute whose life demanded a level of stamina he just could not reach. Trying to please her in other ways, he went into serious debt buying her household items putting him into real difficulty. She complained constantly she needed more money to keep up with other wives living on base. The ever-growing debt only exacerbated the problem, giving her more reasons to criticize him. They were offered marriage counseling but she refused on the grounds she already knew everything one needed to know concerning relationships between a man and a woman. Her response was earthy but realistic, given her street activities as a preparation for marriage. I did not know the couple well enough to determine how solid the marriage was but I was told there was very little promise for this marriage under any circumstances. Regardless, in response to the phone call, I dropped the paper and drove to the bridge. When I arrived, a rather large crowd was standing around waiting to see if Jimmy would actually jump. The crowd gathered around the bridge reminded me of the old western movies when town folk would gather near an elevated platform to see a man hanged. Similar to those crowds, there was a lot of whispering and head shaking in this crowd. The size of the group was large enough to be of concern to the police. From a distance, I could see Jimmy standing on top of the bridge. I asked if someone had notified his wife and was told she arrived about fifteen minutes before me and was standing at the bridge entrance about twenty yards away from Jimmy. I elbowed my way through the crowd, planning to encourage Jimmy to come down from the bridge, share his problem and reach a more reasonable solution than suicide. It was obvious he was infatuated with her. However, should she ask for another chance, he would come down immediately.

Arriving at the bridge, I could see her standing at the end of the bridge yelling something at him. Everyone else in the crowd was absorbed in what she was screaming but I was too far away to hear her comments distinctly. Pushing my way through the crowd I came up behind her. I could hear her screaming in a loud high pitched voice "Jump, Jimmy, jump! You ain't got the guts, Jimmy. That's all you're good for, Jimmy, jump! Go on, jump!" Before I could reach him, jump he did. I ran to the guard rail, jumped over it and slid down the embankment expecting to find Jimmy smashed on the cement highway with cars trying to avoid hitting him. On his way down, Jimmy's foot caught the branch of a small tree sticking out from under the bridge. It caught the leg of his trousers and slammed him into the embankment. He tumbled down the remainder of the embankment and slid onto the pavement. He suffered numerous cuts and bruises and perhaps a broken bone or two. As I reached his side, I heard him say, "I can't even kill myself right." Lucky for him, he was correct. The crowd, having satisfied their curiosity, including his wife, quietly disappeared. An ambulance arrived shortly after the incident and took him to the hospital for observation and treatment. The Navy medical team gave him appropriate treatment and wrapped up his wounds at the base medical facility. He needed medical treatment, but they both needed psychological care. I got up, brushed the dirt off my trousers and returned home; the coffee was cold and the paper waiting to be read.

I never saw Jimmy or his wife again. I presume this event ended their marriage and Jimmy would be transferred to a medical facility where he could get both medical and psychological assistance. I always hoped she took her street values somewhere other than near a military base. One good result of this attempted suicide was its effect on other newly married enlisted personnel living in base housing. They realized cars, washers, dryers and other household goods were not displays of their love. Problems in marriages continued to happen as young, married couples brushed up against differences that can irritate but not destroy a married life founded on respect for each other and a commitment to bringing God into the relationship. At times, occurrences like this happen and when they do, they serve as a reminder that their love for one another is the foundation of their married lives. Other things like household furnishings play a role in their lives but do not determine the quality of their relationship. My experience is military families are solid and well managed. It was always a privilege to be a part of their lives.

Creature of the night

My home was in a new section of town. The contractor had just completed the home for use by his family. It had not been previously lived in. I had a fence, a little more than six feet high encircling the entire back yard. Beyond the fence the desert stretched for miles. Desert growth covered the ground but no trees or large bushes were visible anywhere. Since growing grass in that climate was next to impossible, I bought bags full of colored stones and designed a pattern for the back yard leaving a passageway to the far corner of the yard where I placed a statue of our Blessed Mother. When the temperature cooled down in the evening, I would set on a lawn chair in the back yard reading, resting and watching the universe God created with the Big Bang. This quiet time was seldom broken allowing soft music from my living room to fill the air making it easy to rest or fall asleep. The privacy was almost alive. Living on the last row of houses in this subdivision, a bright moon gave us an unencumbered view of the desert. Given the location of my house, occasionally desert animals would be active outside the fence but none of them ever attempted to enter my yard.

One evening, sitting on a lawn chair on the back porch, I turned off the porch light and found the sky teeming with stars surrounding a pale white moon. Night had settled in leaving us with very little light obscuring most things in the back yard. The temperature was cool and dry - perfect for my purposes. I sat down in my lounge chair, leaned back and began to relax watching the stars flicker and remembering how great their distance was from earth. I reflected on our distance from the stars. We talk in terms of light years. (One light year is equal to six trillion miles). It is difficult to grasp so great a distance. It did remind me this huge unfathomable universe could not have created itself. Some unfathomable power must have created all of this. For most of us this would be God. Some scientists calculated that for one of us to exist today by chance is a ratio of four hundred trillion to one.

This theory supports the principle "nothing cannot create something"- an equation making belief in the existence of God most compelling.

Gradually, I had a strange feeling I was not alone. Something unknown had become a part of my evening. A bit concerned, I slowly turned around looking at the gate leading to the north side of my house, to see if someone was standing there or moving toward me. I probably expected to see some person breaking into my yard. I had weapons but they were inside the house so I was ill prepared to move into some defensive mode. Relieved, I saw no one and determined a twig or other inanimate object must have fallen into my back yard. I rested my head on the back of my chair. However, this uneasy feeling someone or something was in the yard continued to bug me. Then, I thought it must have been something outside my yard, perhaps one of the desert creatures looking for food just passing by. Believing it was probably my imagination, I began again to relax and lean back on my chair. This awareness, however, stayed and began to disturb me. I made a quick survey of the yard. I knew we had poisonous snakes in the area so I scanned the stones looking for a snake slithering toward me. The presence of snakes was not the answer. However, out of the corner of my eye I saw something moving slowly, hugging the fence working his way to the back fence. I knew he was watching me intently could see his eyes glistening from the kitchen light. For a while, it appeared to be a dark colored animal, perhaps a big cat trying to stay concealed from my vision. He never took his eyes off me as he reached the back fence and slowly moved toward the center of the fence. Each step was deliberate as if it were moving into a more advantageous attack position. As it moved along the back fence, the light from the kitchen window made me immediately aware this was no house cat. I did not move a muscle. Actually, I could not move a muscle. Having grown up in Northern Michigan I knew a bobcat, if that is what it was, could be as dangerous as a lion when he decides to attack. I knew he could rush at me and tear me to pieces. Having no defensive weapons within reach, I decided to be absolutely still to ensure the cat would not think I was going to take some aggressive action. When he reached the center of the fence he stopped and looked back at me. I prayed he would be able to crawl up the fence and move out of my yard. The height of the fence made me doubt the cat could jump that high and I knew there were no protrusions on the sides of the fence it could catch on its way. I watched as he got into a crouch and in one jump reached the top of the six foot fence, slid over it and dropped to the ground on the other side. My first instinct was to get in the house as quickly as possible and pick up my 45 caliber weapon load it and put it on the kitchen table in case the cat had a partner less interested in leaving my yard. I concluded my evening with a prayer of sincere thanks for concluding this incident peacefully.

The street I lived on was named Sunrise. It probably had twenty or so homes many of which were occupied by military personnel with a number of civilian families employed at the base. Barstow was not a California entertainment center though there were restaurants, gas stations, bars, grocery stores, clothing stores, desert bicycle riding, and golf. Most of the commercial businesses were located relatively close to Route 66. Given our closeness to Las Vegas some of our recreation included visits to Vegas to gamble for a few hours. I always set a limit to the amount I would spend on the tables. I think it was $20. With the exception of my first visit, I never left the area a big winner. One great advantage I had at the Tropicana was I knew John Garber personally when he was the manager of the casino King's Gateway, a major resort on the borders of Wisconsin and Upper Michigan. At that time I managed a summer camp a few miles from the casino. Some of us would visit the casino when time allowed, and frequently enough to be well acquainted with John. While I was stationed in Barstow, he was one of the managers of the Tropicana Hotel and Casino in Las Vegas. On a number of occasions, when I and some friends went to Las Vegas to play the tables, I would visit him and introduce the friend, several of whom he already knew. Occasionally he would give us tickets to the shows and his personal card with a note on it saying "take care of my friends, John." His card gave us an unreal status. On one occasion my brother Norbert was visiting me. Norb and the assistant from the local parish drove to Vegas for an evening meal and show. Norbert also knew John so we stopped to say hello. John suggested we have dinner at the casino and gave us his card with his note on it. The club was packed when we walked in. We were sure there was no seating available. But we gave the maître-d John's card. He called one of the servers, had a brief discussion and said, please wait a minute. Within a few minutes, there was scurrying around the front of the stage. A table went up, was dressed, and we were escorted to the best table in the house. To avoid abusing his friendship, we did not do this often but whenever we did visit him he made it a memorable occasion. So many of our best memories of Vegas include times when John stepped in with his assistance.

Army Family Accident

An incident took place that probably could happen to any family with children. An Army wife and three children were making a trip to join her husband at his new duty station, Camp Irwin, located in the Mohave Desert not far from Barstow, California. They had been travelling for a considerable spell and the children became rambunctious with a little poking, hair pulling and accusations that they were being messed with and mom wanted whoever to stop it. Driving in the front seat, she could not see what was actually taking place in the back seat. After numerous admonitions to stop the fighting she turned around in her seat to see for herself who was making all the trouble. When she did this she pulled the steering wheel to the right, driving the car off the road, hitting a mound of sand and tipping the car to its side. Miraculously, no one was hurt although all of them could have been injured. Other cars driving near the accident stopped to assist them and one of them being aware of the Barstow Marine Base picked them up and drove them to our facility. Our medical staff examined them determined no one was injured and released them to their own custody. I received a call from the medical center and was asked if I could be of help. I picked them up, drove to my office and discussed what had happened. It proved fortunate she was not speeding and that the car did not completely roll over. Discovering they were army related personnel, we decide to call the Army Emergency Service, and ask for their assistance. I told them about the accident ensuring them there were no serious injuries and they needed transportation to the base and someone to go to the scene of the accident to retrieve their household goods and the car. They responded affirmatively, asked to talk to the mother and discussed what arrangement would be made. The Army base was relatively close by so they came and took over the care of the family and their transportation in a matter of a few hours. I never did find out what happened after they left my office. My concern was that during their absence from the area of the accident, their possessions would be stolen and the car may be un-repairable. I had seen so many serious accidents with loss of life and total destruction of the vehicle, I felt grateful no one was seriously injured.

Life in Barstow

Living in Barstow proved to be a great assignment especially since Jack Gillen and Joe Paquette lived there with their families. While serving together on Okinawa, they shared quarters next to mine and we developed a great friendship that has lasted to this day. Joe's wife was a southern lady who had a family recipe for pecan pie that was unmatched in the universe. Whenever I would get an invitation to drop by and sample her pecan pie I always had the courtesy not to arrive before she hung up the phone but did arrive shortly thereafter. Jack's home was much the same. Invites to dinner were always most welcome. I recall one occasion when Jack's daughter, Kathy, was preparing to participate in her first formal function. I decided to surprise her with her first corsage. I drove to their house and arrived just as they were putting on the final touches of her dress. With Marge's help I pinned on the corsage and stepped back to see if it was placed correctly. Kathy was beautiful without the corsage but it did add a little sophistication to her evening dress. She was surprised and delighted. Jack, Joe and I have continued our friendship since the first day we met at the officer's quarters in Okinawa.

Six Marines killed in a car accident

The Barstow exit from HWY 66 was well maintained with a speed limit of twenty-five miles an hour. It was the exit I used nearly every day during my tour. One evening, two cars–one with four Marines and the other with three–were returning to town when one of them decided to beat the other car load of Marines to the Barstow entrance ramp.

Fully engaged in the competition, they ignored the speed limit and reached the ramp at the same time, side by side. The design of the entrance ramp allowed the entrance of only one car at a time. However, in this case, both cars tried to drive up the ramp first. One of the cars bumped into the other and both cars lost control. Each of them turned over several times. They probably did not have seat belts on, so some were flung out of the cars and onto the soft sand bordering the ramp. People driving by the accident stopped to help. They called the police and almost immediately police and ambulance sirens were heard rushing to the scene. They arrived to find a gruesome scene of bodies and destroyed cars with some still in the car while others lay outside the car half buried in the sand piled up by the accident. When the police, wreckers and ambulances arrived, the bodies were lifted into the ambulances and prepared for the trip to the hospital. As the wrecker began to pull the cars to the side of the road, someone noticed a hand sticking out of the sand. He yelled for help and all the emergency personnel ran to the sand pile and began digging furiously with their hands to free whoever was buried there, hoping to find him alive. The Marine was totally covered by sand with only his hand showing. In seconds they reached him and lifted him out and into one of the ambulances. On the way to the medical center, they managed to bring the Marine back to life. That evening, six Marines were killed and one, who was buried in the sand, lived.

One thoughtless moment and an accident forever changed the lives of seven young Marines. They were out of high school for a few years; just messing around before they returned to their barracks. The base offers driver safety training classes but, like many others, some give very little attention to the lessons after they leave the class room. When several of them are in a car, absorbed in talking about pressing subjects like how much their drill sergeant loved them or the pretty gal at a bar who was too smart to go for a ride with them, or other pressing matters demanding their attention. Concentration on driving skills and safety matters seldom reaches their conscious minds. It was not that they were screw-ups because they weren't. They were just out taking a drive when one of them decided to beat the other to the entrance ramp. No thought was given to the design of the ramp or the low speed limit required for entrance or a thought that an accident could happen. Caution is often forgotten when other interests takeover. In this case, it took the lives of six Marines. The thought that their parents or wives must be notified finds the chaplain or other authority searching for words to use that must break this news to them as gently as possible. You know they will want to know how they died. Saying they were racing another car that resulted in a car accident is the truth but seldom is that explanation appropriate. They will want to know where, how, why this happened. They want to hear that their son or husband died nobly. The truth would devastate them. Generally, saying that the cause of the accident is under investigation is acceptable for the moment. Eventually, they will find out; someone will tell them what really happened. Being able to accept the death of a son or daughter will take a while and in many cases the truth will never be fully accepted.

I learned a great lesson while serving in the Cathedral in Marquette, Michigan when one of our seniors in Catholic Central HS was killed in a single car accident. The time was well into the night when he sped down a paved road that ran along Lake Superior and ended with a ninety degree turn to the right. At the speed he was travelling he attempted the turn but rolled the car into the bushes at the end of the street failing to make a right angle turn. He was killed instantly and taken to the hospital while further arrangements could be made. The police notified the pastor of his parish, Msgr. Casanova, explained what had happened and asked if he would notify the parents. He agreed to do it. To get this message in the wee hours of the morning would be a shock to anyone, especially to a parent being told that their young son, who they loved dearly, had been killed. When he called the family instead of telling them that their son had been killed, he told them their son had been in a serious car accident and he had been taken to St. Mary's Hospital, adding that he would meet them there. For the following minutes the parents driving to the hospital were able to adjust to the results of the accident. In their minds there was the possibility and hope that he would survive but also aware that he may not have survived the crash. When they reached the hospital Msgr. Casanova was waiting for them and then told them that he had died. By that time they had come to accept the reality that he may not have survived the crash. This process of notification eased the acceptance of the tragedy allowing them to mentally adjust to that possibility before they had to accept the reality. Very often there is no time for approaching the problem in this manner. However, in this case and many others, it has been a more humane method of delivering really bad news.

I vividly recall another activity that took place on occasion. Msgr. Casanova's mother lived with him at the parish rectory. Fortunately, in the back yard of the rectory there were several patches of mushrooms growing with no one picking and eating them. During one of our conversations I mentioned how much I loved mushrooms fried in butter. She suggested I visit their rectory, pick the mushrooms and she would prepare them for both of us. The first thing she had to do was teach me to recognize those safe to eat. On some afternoons, I would call Mgr.'s mother, who loved them as much as I did, and ask her if I could drop by and pick some of the mushrooms. She always agreed and I would drive to the rectory, pick a bowl of mushrooms and bring them to her. When I entered the back door with the mushrooms she would have the frying pan on the stove ready to fry them in butter. Although we shared them, I could have eaten all of them myself.

Confirmation of Children of Military Personnel

Sacrament of Confirmation is a major step in our spiritual growth as it strengthens our ability to meet spiritual challenges of adult life. Generally, this sacrament is received while the child is in high school or in the upper levels of primary school. At times, attending the necessary training is difficult for military personnel given their assignments, transfers, available housing, etc. When the children attend a Catholic school, they will receive this sacrament with the other children of that school. However, the tuition at Catholic and private schools generally makes it impossible for many military families to take advantage of the Catholic school system. The only real option we had was to do some intensive training for several weeks during their summer vacation following the end of the scholastic school year. The parish in Barstow, St. Joseph, had a grade school which fortunately, was staffed with religious sisters. I visited the parish pastor requesting him to allow the sisters to come on base to train the children of our military families. He approved and the sisters were happy to help. Preparation involved two weeks of intensive training using the chapel as the training center.

While we were preparing our Marine Corps children, the families at Ft. Irvin, an Army base located in the Mohave Desert near us, was conducting the same training program. So I invited the army children to join us for our confirmation ceremony. Since the children to be confirmed were children of military families, it seemed appropriate to invite Bishop Furlong of the Military Ordinariate to confirm our children. He accepted and arrangements were made for his transportation. Saturday was selected for the ceremonies. Every effort was made to ensure this would be a memorable occasion. Parents decorated the chapel, organized the procession to the chapel and ensured that the children were aware that there would be no clowning around. Needless to say, we did not succeed at 100%. An altar boy led the procession carrying a cross we borrowed from the Barstow parish. The twenty-five or so children to be confirmed followed. The Army chaplain from Ft. Irwin and I led the Bishop into the chapel. Each child had a sponsor who sat with the child during the ceremonies and joined them as they received the sacrament. As the procession entered the chapel, everyone stood and sang a hymn selected for the ceremony. Parents and friends were already seated, waiting for the ceremony to begin. The Bishop offered introductory prayers and then gave a sermon on the importance this sacrament had in their lives and the need to attend Mass and receive the sacrament of reconciliation often as they grew to adulthood. The sermon was directed appropriately toward the parents as well as to the children.

Bishop Furlong, as the Director of the Military Ordinariate, was fully conscious of the difficulties encountered by military families making serious efforts to live their faith fully while serving in the Armed Forces. Although most elements of military life are much the same as they are in civilian life, circumstances in military life make such efforts more difficult. It is the responsibility of the parents to manage them. But it is also calls for the chaplain to make such effort less onerous by assisting as appropriate. Arranging for the Sacrament of Confirmation is an important step in that direction. Bishop Furlong, being fully aware of such factors in military life, addressed them in his sermon encouraging the parents to recognize opportunities in which their children can grow in their faith and make the teaching of Jesus Christ a part of their daily lives. Dozens of other circumstances affecting family life become issues families must encounter and resolve. Preparations for marriage, baptisms, reconciliation, assisting families having marriage problems, including dealing with children reacting adversely for any numbers of reasons are all occasions when turning to God is a prudent and necessary recourse.

During the ceremony, the Bishop stood in the middle of the sanctuary. Each child approached the Bishop and knelt; the sponsor put his or her hand on the shoulder of the child while the Bishop prayed over the child, anointing each of them with holy chrism. The ceremony was a truly impressive, reverent, happy experience. The children were absolutely beautiful; full of excitement and they thoroughly enjoyed being the center of the attention. Pictures were taken of everyone, including parents and friends, who shared their children's joy. Even the chaplains got into some of the pictures.

Following the ceremony, a reception was held when all the parents were given an opportunity to meet Bishop Furlong and welcome him aboard. Bishop Furlong stayed with us for several hours, met with General Nickerson and then had to return to Los Angeles to catch his flight back to Washington. So much of a chaplain's life involves working with adults; it is refreshing to be able to spend time with parents and their children.

Sergeant Herbert

During the Bishop's visit to confirm our children, Sergeant Herbert, always a squared away Marine, was his driver. His family included his wife and two boys, one in high school and the other in the fifth or sixth grade and a dog they loved dearly. Sergeant and his family took the family car, a Volkswagen, to travel out of Barstow to spend the Marine Corps Birthday celebration with friends. The celebration ended in the evening and they left for home. When they left the party, it was already dark. Sergeant had a long day and began dozing off making efforts to stay awake. Finally, unable to stay awake, he went to sleep and lost control of the car as it left the road and hit roughage alongside the highway. In an effort to make a correction he pulled the driving wheel, overcorrected the turn and rolled the car over killing everyone in the family (including the family dog) except for his oldest son Don, who escaped with no serious injury. Don was transported to the medical facility on our base where he was examined and found to have no medical problems.

I was at home when the phone rang. One of the hospital staff members was calling to tell me there had been a car accident involving the Herbert family. Sergeant was French and pronounced his name "aber." I did not recognize the name Herbert but hurried to the hospital to do whatever I could to help out. When I walked into the building I was surprised to see to see Don, the eldest son sitting alone in the examination room. Not recognizing the Herbert name, I asked him "What are you doing here." He answered "Father, we had a car accident coming home from the Marine Corps Birthday celebration and the whole family has been killed." Then it dawned on me. The hospital gave me the English pronunciation of Hebert not the French "aber." So I failed to recognize the family name. Don told me about the accident, how his mom, sitting on the passenger side of the car, was crushed when the car turned over landing on her side of the car. Sergeant was seriously hurt and did not survive the crash; the youngest son lived for a short period but he also died. Don added "Even our dog was killed." I had difficulty expressing my feelings for the loss of such a great friend and his family. I stayed with him for a while. His relatives came to the base and took Don with them. The thought came to me Marines die in battle not in some family car accident. But, the longer I worked with the Marines, the more realistic my grasp of Marine life changed as it was evident Marines, like other citizens, die like everyone else and for the same reasons. I know we continually discuss in our sermons that we should live our lives realizing we could meet our Maker at any time. It seems death arrives unexpectedly, even to those with terminal illness.

However, at times death is desired. I remember visiting a retirement home with my brother, also a priest. He offered Mass once a month in a reception area of the retirement facility. I went with him and, after Mass; we were talking with the residents about the deer hunting season and some of the other winter sports absorbing our TV time. At one point an older gentleman (90 year old) asked Father Norb if it was alright to pray to die. Norb said it certainly was alright to do so. I looked at the man and told Norb he did not seem to be happy and actually looked healthier than either of us. This took place some years ago so I imagine, by this time, his prayers would have been answered.

A serious car/train accident

A week or so after returning from vacation, I was doing some work at the chapel. A radio was on and I was listening to the news when the program was interrupted to say there had been a serious auto accident in which all three of the occupants had been killed. One of which was a member of the military stationed in Barstow, California. Apparently, the car ran into a train killing all the occupants. Within a few minutes after the radio announcement, my phone rang. Headquarters was calling me to attend a special meeting to discuss actions to be taken immediately. When I arrived, the Commanding Officer and several others were standing together discussing the course of action they would take. Since the accident involved an active duty sailor on shore duty, several factors require immediate action. One of which was the notification of the sailor's wife or next of kin. In this case, several complex issues were of concern as the accident involved the sailor, his father and grandfather. When I reported in, I was given additional information about the accident. The deceased sailor was stationed at our base. And then, as if to make the tragedy worse, we were told the sailor, his dad and his grandfather were the occupants of the car. The accidental death of a sailor, especially at his home base, is always a tragedy. The death of the sailor, his dad and his grandfather is a catastrophe. His personnel file listed his family address as Los Angles, Ca. It was determined his wife and other family members were presently at that address. As the base CACO officer (Casualty Assistance Officer) I was responsible for personally notifying the family of the accident and offering to assist them as much as I could. I asked Sergeant Malic from communications if he would go with me. He said yes and we left immediately.

We arrived in Los Angles toward early evening. It was still light enough to find the address without difficulty. We drove around the area to find the street. When we found it, we made a left turn and started to drive toward the address of the family. The street had very little activity. When we entered it we were over several blocks from the family home. Even from this distance, we could see three women, arms around each other and looking at our approaching car. They did not move an inch. They just stood there fearing the car they saw approaching slowly toward them was coming to give them news they did not want to hear. As we drove nearer to them, they were holding hands, crying, fearing the accident they had heard about on the news involved their husbands. Hoping against hope, they saw their worst fears were about to be verified. They stood together, eyes fixed on us as we drove toward them. When we came to a stop in front of their home, they burst into tears, hugging each other to share their hurt, having confirmed their fears had come true. As I opened the car door we heard sobbing and voices saying "No, no it can't be." As we walked toward them, we could feel the sense of fear and loss enveloping all three women. Their worst fears had happened and we were there to verify the tragedy. Their overwhelming sorrow touched us deeply, making it difficult to deliver the information on the accident or even express our regrets for their loss. They were experiencing pain so deep they were unable to raise their heads. I walked up to them knowing what I should say but feeling so devastated like them at first that I was unable to express it. The hurt they felt was overwhelming as they tried to console each other. In the yard, I told them what had happened and suggested we move into the house where they could sit while I gave them the information. When we had moved into the house, I gave them the information made available to me and told them further details would be given to them once the investigation was completed. Although I discussed the information on the assistance the Navy would give the sailor's family, I am sure they never consciously heard what I said. I was not too concerned because there would be immediate follow-up contacts by naval personnel to discuss issues that needed to be explained and answers given to the many questions absorbing their thoughts. I have had to deliver death messages in the past but none ever concerned three immediate relatives killed together in one car accident. After spending some time with the family, we knew it was time to leave and return to base.

As we walked away from the home, the sergeant and I felt the terrible sense of loss this family was experiencing and the sense of hopelessness that could not be corrected or undone. To lose a son or husband or grandfather is serious enough, but to lose all three at one time, in one accident in the same family, is unfathomable. I do not recall being involved in any incident so filled with a sense of loss from which there was no escape. The unbelievable had taken place and it happened during our watch.

Visit by my family while stationed in Barstow

While serving with the Marines in Barstow, California. I had the good fortune to have my parents and two of my sisters visit me for a couple of weeks. My sister Rita was my older sister and Patty was in High School. Being stationed at a base with hundreds of young Marines gave Pat opportunities to date them during her stay. The weather was perfect, allowing us to travel around southern California which included a visit to Disney World and to the Capistrano Mission, famous for the annual return of the cliff swallows on March 19, the feast day of St. Joseph. The return of the swallows on March 19 has been taking place for the past 200 years.

A characteristic of Barstow weather is that it is very dry. My mother had a severe case of rheumatoid arthritis which in damp weather would heighten the pain. After a few days in Barstow's dry desert weather, for the first time in years the pain in her joints was seriously reduced. Our neighbors could not have been nicer. General Nickerson's wife had an afternoon tea for my folks, demonstrating the courtesy for which she was well known. I thought it would be great for them to stay in Barstow and take over my home. However, events followed that changed that possibility. My sister Rita had not felt well for some weeks but made the trip believing she would return to normal in the immediate future. Instead, she became increasing exhausted and decided to fly home to Chicago to check in with her doctor. The diagnosis was not good. She had developed myeloma cancer and was told she only had a few weeks to live. Arrangements were made immediately to fly my dad and mom to Chicago while Pat and I would drive there with the car. We drove as long as we could but had to stop for one night's rest. When we reached Texas, Pat took over the driving and I gave her one admonition. "Don't run out of gas. The distance between gas stations is so great it could leave us with a real serious problem." She agreed and I sat on the passenger side and fell sound asleep. Suddenly, the car started to become jerky and slowed down. I woke up with a start and asked what had happened. She said: "I'm sorry, but I think we ran out of gas." I just about panicked. Looking up on the right side of the road about one hundred yards ahead was a gas station, lights on and still open. I ran to the station borrowed a can for some gas, poured it in the car and drove the car to the station for a fill-up. Our habit of praying for a safe trip was richly rewarded. We were able to reach Chicago in order to spend a little time with Rita before she passed on.

Although there were some difficult events during my tour, my time in Barstow will be recalled with memories of great friends, many kindnesses, luck in Vegas and the opportunity to manage a great parish for two years.

Germany & Spain

During my eight years in the Navy, I travelled both in and outside the USA. For example, when I had some annual leave available, I would go to Edwards Air Force Base and ask what flights they had scheduled to go anywhere. If there was a flight to a location I wanted to visit and if there was room for me on the aircraft, I would sign in, go back to the base, pack my travel bag and join the crew. Some of the trips proved to be well worth the time spent. Just a few moments on two of them will give you an idea of what I experienced.

I had enough earned leave to travel for several weeks. As usual I went to Edwards Air Force Base to see if I could hitch a ride to one of their destinations. The staff at Edwards was always courteous and helpful. I asked what flights they had going anywhere in the world. Fortunately, the officer in charge suggested I catch the Inspector General's flight because it was leaving the next day for Berlin, Germany and it would make several stops that would prove interesting, especially being able to evaluate the East and West Berlin cultures. The cold war was active and a trip to Berlin would definitely prove exciting. I returned to Barstow, packed some clothes and the next morning hurried back to Base for the trip to Europe. Our plane had just started rolling down the runway when an arriving Air Force aircraft notified our crew we had a flat tire. We stopped and an emergency crew came to the rescue and within a half hour we were back on the runway continuing our flight to Germany. Given the distance we were to travel and the size of our aircraft, it was necessary to make a few stops to refuel. We made four refueling stops beginning with the stop at Wright Patterson, Ohio; then Newfound, Scotland and Freiberg Germany before flying to Berlin. I wanted to add a few paragraphs about this visit because it had such a profound impact on my understanding of communism in practice, seeing it lived rather than hearing of its failures.

Freiburg, Germany, a city with a formidable US Armed Forces Command, was our destination for this leg of our trip. We spent very little time there, stopping to refuel and we continued our trip to Berlin. While there waiting, I stood next to an Air force pilot. He looked at all the areas of the airport like he was trying to refresh his memory. Then he leaned over to me and whispered "I bombed the shit out of this place." I believed him as damage from the bombing was still visible in some areas of the airport. Our route to Berlin took us over East Germany, occupied by the Soviets since the end of WWII. The landscape was barren with an almost total absence of people anywhere, exhibiting the Soviet reconstruction efforts. Houses appeared to be unoccupied; no cars or trucks moved along the highway nor did we see working farms with cattle grazing in the fields. The inability or unwillingness of the Communist leadership to assist in the recovery of East Germany was visible everywhere. The land looked cold, uninviting and lifeless. The fly-over convinced me life in a communist country like East Germany would be miserable at best.

East Germany had a way of life governed by the Soviet military determined to punish Germany for the destruction of Europe and specifically those who left Russia in shambles. Life in East Germany became so unacceptable citizens of East Germany began moving out of the East into West Germany where reconstruction was in full force and living conditions were returning to normal. To stop the flow west, a wall was built to prevent this westward movement. East Germans who braved crossing the border, were shot to death while attempting to make the move. More than nine hundred East Germans were killed attempting to cross into West Germany. There were no major growth activities or industry, and definitely no improvement in their standard of living. Communist governance of industrial operations was dismal. An example is the operation of a power plant in East Germany. During the Soviet occupation they employed a workforce of twenty thousand employees. When the Wall came down and Western German management procedures were employed the workforce was reduced to two thousand employees.

Soviet Blockade and Berlin Airlift

To hinder, if not stop, the progress being made in West Germany under the care of the Allies, on June 22, 1948, Russia cut off all ground transportation to Berlin. They were unable to restrict air transportation as this was protected by International law. This restrictive control could have been a disaster to Berlin since the city was located about 170 miles into East Germany and was encircled by Russian occupational forces. Travel by air was the only method available to reach the Tempelhof Airport in Berlin. On June 28, 1948, to counter the Russian travel restrictions, the Allies, primarily the USA, developed an airlift that carried supplies over the "hump" from Rheims Main, an Air force base near Frankfort, Germany, to Berlin. At first glance, the needs of the city were so severe it appeared to be an impossible task. Then General Lemay was assigned to develop an Air Force system that would meet the supply needs of West Berlin. He did this and beat all odds. To begin the airlift, he brought in one hundred aircraft known as the "Gooney Birds (C-41)). They proved that supplies could be delivered by air to Berlin efficiently. They were able to haul two thousand tons a day. General May then requested larger planes, (the C-54 Sky master) that carried four times the amount of supplies than did the "Gooney Birds." Ultimately, the Allies flew three hundred tons of food and other supplies a day into West Berlin. The volume of air traffic was so huge that aircraft were given three minutes to slip into the airport after the plane before them landed. If the plane was not able to meet the three minute timing, it had to return to base with its load of supplies. Berlin needed everything, from food and medicine to coal and fuel. The crews that flew the coal eventually developed problems from the coal dust that permeated the aircraft. The Berlin Airlift was about the biggest relief service ever attempted and the success of this effort is now a part of history.

Realizing their blockade did not stop the Allies from meeting the needs of the Berliners; Russia rescinded its prohibition on the use of ground transportation and the operation returned to normal. The Berlin Airlift delivered over 2.3 million tons of food and other supplies. Additionally, the Berlin Air lift demonstrated the magnanimity of the American people and our allies to rise above their hurt and relieve the pain of a former enemy. An activity that surprised Germans was the trust the Allied Air Force placed in them by hiring former German Air Force machinists and other aircraft personnel to repair allied aircraft. There were so many aircraft used for the Berlin Air lift that the Allied Forces did not have a sufficient number of trained personnel to manage aircraft repair needs. The participation of the German machinists and others helped keep the supply flights operating.

A story that touched the hearts of the world was the practice of Lt. Halvorsen, a pilot who was a part of the flight crews moving supplies into Tempelhof Airport. He met some of the children who hung out around the fence at the airport and gave some of them bags of gum and candy. The lieutenant was so pleased with the children's gratitude that he decided to put candy in bags tied to handkerchiefs and parachute them to the children as he entered the airport for a landing. Planes were landing every three minutes so they asked him how they could tell it was his airplane; he told them he would wiggle the wings on his plane. This practice earned the lieutenant the name "Uncle Wiggly Wings." Soon after, other pilots did the same thing. This practice continued throughout the Berlin Airlift. It would be impossible to know how many German people were saved during the airlift but it must have been thousands. When our plane landed in West Berlin, our world changed. Lights lit up streets and homes, restaurants, stores; streets looked much like a city in the US. People were shopping, walking freely, smiling, and enjoying the freedom brought to them by the Allied Forces. The atmosphere was relaxed and the service courteous. I joined some of the Air Force Chaplains for dinner at a club a few miles from the Air Force barracks. They selected the meal and drinks. The dinner entrée was a "hasenpfeffer" (rabbits) with all the trimmings, a really excellent meal. The drink we ordered "Altbierbowle" was German beer mixed with strawberry juice. It proved to be a great drink that went perfectly with any meal as well as with many other activities where beer is an appropriate beverage. Although I have looked for places that sold this beer, I have not been able to find one. I could try to make one myself but I have no idea what the mixture would include. While we were at the restaurant, each table had a phone available to call and talk to patrons in other booths. I noticed that the system was working for several people. I waited to see if someone in a booth left it and went to another booth to meet the person with whom he or she had been talking. I did not see any movement while we were eating dinner but it seemed to be an easy way to make new acquaintances.

The dinner broke up and I decided to walk to Brandenburg Gate which separated East and West Berlin. The sun was setting, giving buildings in East Berlin an eerie, foreboding appearance. Except for the guards at the gate, I did not see even one person or any movement on the East side of the gate. That part of the city was as lifeless as a cemetery. Ordinarily, I would have tried to find someone who could give me permission to go into East Berlin. This time I had absolutely no desire to cross the border.

Trip to Seville Spain famous for its Flamenco Dancers, Spring Festivals, and Bull Fights

As I made preparations for my return trip, I discovered that there was an Air Force flight leaving for Seville, Spain that afternoon. I still had time left on my leave, so I managed to join the flight crew for the trip. Seville proved to be outstanding in every way. This was my first trip to Seville. While serving on the *Shangri-La* some years later, I was able to return to Seville during the Feria de April festival and participate in city-wide celebrations.

I was told that Seville is the port from which Columbus sailed to discover the Americas. It was a thoughtful time standing on the dock, watching the Guadalquivir River flow out to sea realizing that, in 1492, Columbus sailed out of this Spanish port and discovered our hemisphere. When I reached Seville, I visited the Air Force base and met an Army and an Air Force chaplain; one, a retired Army chaplain, was conducting some research and the other an Air Force chaplain was still on active duty. They shared an apartment in downtown Seville and suggested I stay with them during my visit.

It seemed that the people of Seville spoke several languages. Thankfully, the most frequently encountered were Spanish and English. This apartment entrance emptied into a narrow street just wide enough to allow Father Frank's Citroen automobile to park and other small cars to squeeze by. Most apartments had window balconies with pots of colorful flowers reaching down the side of the buildings nearly touching the walkways. Fragrance from roses, gardenias, and mums filled the air. When Father Frank and I were leaving the building, we met the apartment manager. Frank introduced me and she asked if I spoke Spanish. I said "No." 'French? I answered "A little bit." Does he speak German? My answer was the same: "No." She turned to Father Francis (the retired Army chaplain), shook her head and said "How sad." I had to agree. I had opportunities to learn Spanish and failed to make that effort. If I could have spoken Spanish I would have asked her how the Spanish survived WWII. As a result, I lost many opportunities to delve into Spain's activities in WWII and other life matters that explain the quality of life in this country.

On one of the evenings, we went to a club that served both Spanish and American food. The main course consisted of roasted lamb, rice, asparagus, and garnishments. I remember this dinner for several reasons; the food was excellent and for the first time I had the opportunity to watch Flamenco Dancers. The music was captivating.

The dancers were dressed in black costumes. The precision of their movements, the costumes they wore and the serious features of their faces made this an unforgettable experience. The audience joined in with the musicians by clapping their hands rhythmically along with gestures of the dancers who set the beat by hitting the floor of the stage with the metal heels of their shoes. I was cautioned that if I wanted to clap my hands with the rest of the dinners, to be sure I did so in coordination with the beat of the rest of the audience. The perfection of their movements kept us spellbound; a truly magnificent performance.

Frank volunteered to go on a drive through the Spanish country side to visit some small towns that surrounded Seville. This could not have been a frequent practice for visitors to Spain. Everywhere we went; our appearance took the natives by surprise. On one instance, we parked and took out a Polaroid camera and prepared to take pictures of some children, probably twelve to fifteen years old, watching us. Their curiosity lured them to come closer and meet us. We told them we were Americans and that we worked as chaplains. We asked them if we could take their pictures. They were delighted to pose. We took a number of shots and showed them to the children. Apparently, they had never experienced a camera that could take pictures and develop them within minutes. They appeared to be surprised at how they looked; commenting and pointing to one another with smiles and laugher. We gave them the pictures and continued our sightseeing tour.

ROTA, SPAIN and African trip

Determined to visit as many places as time allowed, I took a train to the naval base near Rota, Spain. The facility served many purposes but one of them was to service American military ships operating in the Atlantic. I spent a couple of days in Rota staying with the base Catholic chaplain. He had familiarized himself with Spanish history, and Spain's struggle with the Moors, a struggle that lasted three hundred years. The Moors struggled with the Christians, killing them and destroying their homes and churches,

The Moors made every effort to move Christians out of the Palestine portion of the Middle East. After countless battles between the Christians and the Muslims, the tide turned favorable for the Christians. The struggles, much like the skirmishes we are experiencing today in the Middle East, were based on the religious beliefs that Christians must be killed.

Being so close to the coast of Africa, we used this opportunity to visit Morocco and spent two days at a hotel in Tangier. It was comfortable and located near the edge of the city. This was the only time a hotel had ever asked for my passport. Late afternoon, we walked around the city, stopping at shops that filled the streets. The architecture was dominated by a Moorish culture although western influences were clearly visible. The temperature was extremely hot. We returned to the hotel, checked out and started driving around the areas outside the city of Tangier and found a place that offered camel rides. Believing this to be the first and possibility the last chance I would have to ride on a camel, it looked like the right thing to do. I paid the fee and waited for the camel to be selected. The manager told me which one to ride. He had the camel lie down and helped me to climb onto the saddle. Expecting the animal to stand up like a horse, I grabbed the saddle as the camel lurched forward, then to the left and then to the right and I found myself hanging on to the saddle to avoid falling off. Then it lowered its head and neck toward the ground while simultaneously raising its backside. A few more maneuvers, and after getting its legs straightened, it rested until given motivation to move out. When it finally stood at its full height, the camel towered over people and the horses grazing in the same location. I was certain that a fall from this height could do some physical damage and make a major dent in my pride. I hung onto the horn of the saddle tightly. It began walking the circle inside the fenced area. The ride was fine but not all that comfortable. Given its manner of walking, it would take some time to find a comfortable way to ride it for any length of time. Other foreigners stood around watching me, determining if they wanted to go through the same exercise. As we left, I resolved that this ride was the last camel ride I would take voluntarily.

After the ride, we walked around the area and found a restaurant. The meal was very good. I faintly remember eating couscous and pastille (pigeon meat, rice and vegetables.) Some of the food was a bit greasy but gave a flavor that made the meal a real treat. We enjoyed the visit and returned to Rota and had a good night's sleep. When the trip came to an end, as usual, I went to the Air Force base near Seville and caught a flight back to the states and to my duty station in Barstow.

USS Shangri-La (CVA 38)

Skyhawk Landing with tail hook lowered
to catch restraining cable.

Crusader being catapulted from Flight deck

Palma Majorca, Spain School Children
visiting the Shangri-La

Crew treating visiting children with
ice cream and cookies.

Cardinal Archbishop Krol consecrating
the chapel on the USS Shangri-La

Instruction in chapel onboard the Shangri-La

Baptism Ceremony

Chapter 16
Aircraft Carrier *Shangri-La* (CVA 38) tour

E ach year, naval officers are given a "Dream Sheet" from which we were to select assignments we would prefer to have in the future. I have always been attracted to aircraft and many years ago I learned to fly in a biplane "Meyers OTW" while living in Marquette, Michigan. On the form, I wrote "Naval Air Anywhere" across the Dream Sheet page. Thankfully, I received an assignment to the aircraft carrier USS *Shangri-La* CVA 38 (*Shang*) anchored at the Philadelphia Navy Ship Yard, where it was undergoing extensive repair and updating.

Although I was anxious to report aboard the *Shangri-La*, I stopped in Wausau, WI. to spend some time with my folks before I continued my trip. My car had a considerable amount of miles but was in relatively good shape. I gave it to my sister who was in high school and bought another car. A friend of mine, a manager with Chevrolet in Detroit, had an Impala Super Sport he'd been driving for a few months. He said the car was available, in excellent condition and had very few miles on it. I could purchase it for the same price he paid for it; about half the dealer's price. I needed a newer car and was happy to have this car, especially at this price. I flew to Detroit, took a cab to his residence, bought the car and began the final leg of my trip. The trip to the Philadelphia Naval Ship Yard took about eight hours; not bad when compared to the trip from Barstow to Wausau, Wisconsin.

On December 3, 1965, I arrived at the Philadelphia Naval Shipyard just as the *Shangri-La* had moved into dry dock for one of her biggest overhauls since she was re-commissioned in 1955. The repair work continued until mid-May.

Until the day I arrived at the Philadelphia Navy Ship Yard, I had never been on a carrier or even close enough to see a ship that size. I was aware that the *Shang* had an excellent service record, taking part in World War I1 when it earned two Battle Stars and her participation in active combat service throughout the Vietnam War during which she earned three more Stars. Reviewing the history of the ship gave an excellent grasp of the important role the *Shang* played in World War II and other combat engagements through the Vietnam Conflict. Its planes took an active role in World War II where she gave support to ground forces, destroying Japanese radio and radar installations. Her flight crew flew combat air patrols and gave close air support for the 10th Army operating on Okinawa. While stationed at Ulithi, an island off the coast of Okinawa, Vice Admiral John S. McCain, Sr., father of Senator John McCain, used the *Shang* as his flagship. From this location, the *Shang* task force launched air strikes on Japanese home islands where its airmen suffered the heaviest casualties. Then in February, 1945, *Shangri-La* pilots attacked Tokyo on several occasions, inflicting serious damage on Japanese industry. Being a late entry into World War II, the *Shang* made up for it by bombing raids on the islands surrounding Japan and ultimately being a major player in the destructive attacks made on Tokyo itself. Planes from the *Shangri-La* conducted so many bombing runs on Tokyo itself and the islands surrounding Japan that the ship received the nickname "Tokyo Express."

It did not take long for me to love sea duty. Given the size of the *Shangri-La*, living on board the ship was similar to living in a medium sized town in the USA.

When I arrived at the shipyard, the *Shangri-La* was docked with dozens of shipbuilders pouring over every inch of the ship. I found a convenient parking space, parked and walked to the ship. I stopped for a few minutes to take in the size of this ship, wondering how long it would take to bring the ship up to its full operational status. For a moment, the ship looked like a bomb had dropped on it. There were cranes, dozens of work areas and what appeared to be hundreds of men working diligently to meet a deadline. I made my way up the ladder to the hanger bay level. I saw some workers in this area and asked where I could find the XO. I was aware the Captain was not onboard. Civilians were working throughout the ship, giving it a complete makeover. Passageways were open for the most part allowing access to major areas of the ship. I found the XO, Commander Waters, introduced myself and handed him a copy of my orders. We discussed the sea duty experience I had on several missions. I mentioned my longest trip was as a passenger on a troop ship from Long Beach, California to Okinawa and that the other trip on board a ship involved the time I spent with the Marines for the three months during the Cuban Crisis, and our participation in South Korea preparing for an invasion by the North Koreans on the 10th anniversary of the signing of the treaty ending the Korean Conflict. Besides fishing from a row boat, my experience on water-going vehicles was limited to watching them pass through the Locks at Sault Saint Marie, Michigan. After introductions, I told him I was happy to be a member of the ship's crew and I was anxious to settle down and begin performing my job. Serving under his command gave me a favorable opinion of him, his leadership and the assistance he gave to make our programs successful. I asked where my quarters were located. The XO assigned me to private quarters, mid-ship, on the deck below the hanger bay close to the officer's mess. This location was perfect as it allowed access for both officers and crew. It was big enough to have a bed, wash basin, a desk and a closet sufficient to hold the clothing I carried with me. Everything I owned fit comfortably in two suitcases and an overnight bag. Before this assignment, I spent four years with the US Marines. So this tour promised to be a whole new, much more comfortable, experience.

Going onboard for the first time, I entered a world of equipment repair with hundreds of ship builders fully occupied with their torches, welders, and hammers, installing ship parts and bringing the ship's computer services up to date. So many people and things were on the move it reminded me of an ant hill with dozens of people engaged in their work, moving about purposefully, bringing the ship to its best condition. The decks were alive with crews busy with tools and cranes, welding and retrofitting equipment and doing a hundred other jobs equally if not more important. The work was being completed in cold weather. Given the extent of the repairs, the ship was open and cold, much like living in a giant refrigerator. There was no heat in the ship including my quarters. Except for sleeping, the cold did not bother me. I grew up in Northern Michigan where, a saying goes, "we have nine months of winter and three months of poor sledding." I knew we had to dress for cold weather and I was prepared. At night, I would bury myself under the covers. During the day my time was spent learning about the ship, its crew and the programs the ship was preparing to undertake. The more time I spent on the ship, the greater my respect grew for the competence required to operate the complexities of an aircraft carrier, specifically the *Shangri-La*. The ship was huge but since I had a two year tour on the *Shang* I made a commitment to myself that I would visit every part of the ship before being transferred to another assignment. By the time I completed my tour, I did not come close to meeting my goal.

Living on a ship while it is undergoing repair took some time to get used to. The noise the shipbuilders was making noise everywhere on the ship. A lesson I learned while on the *Shangri-La* was that noise being made on one section of the ship can be heard at least a hundred feet beyond the area in which the noise is happening. Given the steel structure of the ship, a hammer sticking the deck of the ship in one part of the ship would be heard in another part of the ship and sound as if it happened next to your quarters. An example of this noise transfer happened to me at about 2 A.M. There was a hatch next to my quarters leading down to the ship's ammunition storage location. When transferring ammo to that location the hatch would be opened and the ammo lowered using steel chains to hold the load of ammo being transferred to a lower deck. The chain rubbing against the steel made a very loud sound that would be heard in all the areas adjacent to my quarters. On another occasion, at 2 A.M. I heard a hammer pounding on the deck that I thought was taking place next to my quarters. I got up and searched the passageways around my area and found nothing. In the future, I never bothered to search for the cause of uncommon noises realizing that it was a just another part of daily life aboard a sea-going airport.

Aircraft Carriers Resemble an Airport At Sea

The aircraft carrier Shangri-La is a sea going airport that houses some ninety aircraft, over 3,000 personnel, and enough firepower to inflict serious damage on any target it is assigned to eliminate.

Aircraft are stored on the flight deck and in the hanger bay where aircraft repair takes place. Like any airport, the noise level of aircraft landing and taking off fills every inch of the flight deck and several levels below, making it necessary for flight crews to have double ear protection, ear plugs and earmuffs (cranial protection) to prevent damage to their hearing.

The tremendous roar of exploding steam from the catapult and the blast of an F 8 Navy jet at full throttle sends the aircraft down the flight deck speeding at the rate of 0 to 165 MPH in two seconds. This is truly an awesome experience for the pilot and an unbelievable experience for those fortunate enough to witness this action nearly every day. In many ways, living on an Aircraft Carrier is like living in an airport. The flight deck is alive with planes taking off and landing; crews attaching aircraft to the catapults and a flight deck officer ensuring everything is ready, signals the pilot to launch his aircraft. While this is taking place, other aircraft are landing and being moved out of the way to allow more aircraft to land. Planes are being fueled, loaded with ammunition, and whatever else is needed by the pilot to carry out his mission. The duties of the crew on the flight deck call for quick, heads up actions on the part of all hands to avoid accidents and to make aircraft ready for launching. Although everyone on the flight desk is working in the same space, their duties differ. To ensure that the command and others responsible for a safe and efficient launch and capture of every aircraft, it is important that the members of the crew can be identified by the function they perform. This is accomplished by crew members wearing jackets of a specific color that identifies the functions the member is to perform. There are seven different colors used by crew members working on the flight deck. Each color distinguishes a specific function. These include the following:

Purple-aircraft refueling (better known as grapes)

Blue-aircraft handlers, move planes from the hangar to the flight deck, hook-and-chain men.

Green-worn by the ABH (Aviation Boatswain's Mates) responsible for hooking up cargo, operating catapults and arresting gear.

Yellow - Control, essentially directing aircraft, signaling them, or the people in charge of overall operations.

Brown-plane captains, responsible for ensuring the aircraft for which they are responsible are fully functional and ready to go on any missions assigned.

Red-Ordnance, Crash and Salvage (firefighting teams)

White-Corpsmen (medics), safety observers, plane inspectors.

Loading ammunition onto aircraft, putting planes in positions for launch, attaching the plane to the catapult as other aircraft are landing and being moved to secure areas of the flight deck and dozens of other activities makes the flight deck of an aircraft carrier the most dangerous work place in the country. This entire operation takes place at the same time. Dangerous, but far less so, is the hanger bay, a machine shop that extends practically the full length of the ship's 888 feet. Sailors work around the clock, keeping the ship and its aircraft at the ready. Crews grapple with everything from tires and brakes to the most sophisticated of electronic equipment. However, all the things call for close attention, but especially two of them: ammunition and fuel are at the top of the list. Mishandling either of them could seriously jeopardize the ship and its crew. We carried enough explosives to wipe out our country from Mayport, Florida to Chicago, Illinois. Bombs and other weapons are carefully stored, guarded and always maintained with the highest levels of security. The same is true of fuel management. A carrier will carry 8,500 tons of aircraft fuel and several hundred thousand gallons of fuel to power the ship. The responsibility for fuel and ammunition management is enormous. Except for night flights, the operations of the ship quiet down toward evening as the crew gets some much needed rest.

An aircraft carrier is a huge ship built to conduct combat operations at sea and on land. The *Shang* was an effective, adaptable, multi-tasking fighting ship that could travel at thirty-five knots (forty-three miles an hour) with aircrafts that can reach a speed of sound and highly skilled sailors dedicated to keeping the ship and its aircraft combat ready. At sea there are no easy days.

The carrier handles more aircraft landings and take-offs than most airports and always under far more stressful conditions. Like a small floating town, we had sleeping quarters, a library, and a laundry, chapel, barber shops, movies, stores for shopping and a mess hall (cafeteria) open twenty-four hours that prepares about ten thousand meals a day. Super aircraft carriers are now powered by nuclear fuel, reducing the amount of carbon fuel oil and gas used by carriers in the past. An interesting observation is that our nuclear submarines can spend months submerged without the need to surface because of their nuclear power system.

The Ship's Structure Is an Amazing Feat of Engineering

The ship's hull is constructed of strong, thick steel plates, several inches thick, making it able to withstand battle damage. There is a second inner hull of steel plating with a gap between them to protect against torpedoes or accidents at sea. The flight deck is of prime importance as it is handles the landing and takeoffs of aircraft. The ship serves as an airfield for naval aircraft. The *Shang*'s flight deck was just short of nine hundred feet; approximately the length of three football fields. The width of the deck is 250 feet. The height of the ship from the keel (bottom of the ship) to the mast of the ship is 240 feet, as high as a twenty-four story building. Although the length of the deck is extensive, aircraft landing at speeds of 145 miles an hour are not able to come to a full stop on the length of the flight deck without an arresting mechanism., To do so, the deck has four arresting wires extending across the flight deck to catch a hook extending from the rear end of the aircraft. At times, a plane misses all four wires and has to go around again attempting another landing. Carriers have an angled deck that is used for landings so that if an aircraft misses the wires it can leave the ship without crashing into activities taking place on the forward deck such as other aircraft preparing to launch.

Installation of A Chapel And Its Consecration By Cardinal Arch Bishop John Krol

Preparing to offer Mass, I searched the ship looking for a chapel and soon discovered that the ship did not have one. Since the ship held thousands of sailors, of which at least 83% believed in God and over half of whom came from families that practiced their faith, a chapel would be a great convenience for those wishing to spend a few moments with their Creator. I requested the XO to have a chapel installed. He replied: "Find someone willing to give up some of their space and you can have a chapel installed." That afternoon, I met with the CAG (Commander Air Group) and asked if he would give up a few square feet of his space that we could use as a chapel. He said he would look into it and get back with me. The next day the CAG called saying he would give us some space and gave me the location. The space was neatly located mid-ship on the deck below the hanger bay; it was perfectly located for the convenience of officers and crew. After notifying the XO of the space we received, he contacted the civilian workforce superintendent and let him know of the project we were going to add to their workload. He approved the addition and ordered all the items needed to build the chapel. The pews were flown in from Mayport, Florida. and the Hammond organ was salvaged from the Lake Chaplain during its deactivation. Several other additional conveniences were added but for us the addition of the chapel made all the difference.

Cardinal Arch Bishop John Krol

Fortunately, while the ship was under repair in Philadelphia, I met one of the priests and had time to visit his rectory and spend time with him. I mentioned to him that we were having a chapel installed in the *Shangri-La* and it would be the first chapel an aircraft carrier had ever had. In fact, I believe it was could be the only ship with a full-time chapel. Its importance for offering Mass and administering the sacraments, having baptisms, religious services and instructions etc.

was apparent. We discussed having the chapel consecrated and I admitted I had no idea of who to ask. He said he would ask if Cardinal Krol could fit it in his schedule. The answer was affirmative and one afternoon the Cardinal came onboard with one of his staff and consecrated the chapel; an unbelievable honor.

Philadelphia Cheese Beef Steak

While in the Philadelphia Ship Yard, Don Watts, a great friend, pilot and a member of the Ship's crew, introduced me to the "Philly cheese beef steak sandwich" served at a restaurant a few blocks from the ship's dock. Without any exception, this sandwich was the very best sandwich anywhere in the world. We went there for lunch as often as time allowed. Finally, after being away from Philly for a few decades, I drove to Philadelphia to visit the Liberty Bell and other historic sites. I could not leave the city until I had an opportunity to find a restaurant that served the Philly sandwich. We found it near the shipyards. I ordered one, watched it being made, and once again had the best cheese beef sandwich in the world. No one should visit Philadelphia without eating the Philadelphia cheese beef steak. It will be the highlight of your stay. Don and Jane played a major part in my life while we were stationed in Philadelphia and Mayport, FL. Visiting their home was always like spending time with my family.

Preparation For A Cruise To The Caribbean

Some of the information I found amazing. The aircraft is a floating airport with nearly all the accouterments characteristic of a good sized city. The services needed to keep a city operating are also required in an aircraft carrier with an additional number of utilities and combat related areas such as storage of ammunition, and huge amounts of fuel. Learning about some of the characteristics of a carrier gave me a great respect for the engineers who designed the ship making it able to withstand severe attacks on its hull, flight deck, and other areas of the ship vital to its survival when engaged in battle or fighting waves huge enough to raise the ship's bow out of the water.

Although both landing and launching functions are complex functions, shooting an aircraft off the flight deck is far more problematic. The length of the flight deck is too short for the jet aircraft like the F8 with a loaded weight of 29,000 lbs. to use as a runway like those found on land airports. To assist the plane into the air, the flight deck has catapults designed to hook a tow bar on the front of the plane that assists the plane with enough pressure to get the plane airborne. When it is ready for launch, the catapult officer (shooter) ensures the amount of pressure is sufficient for the specific aircraft and signals the takeoff procedures to start. The pilot puts the plane at full throttle and the catapult bursts simultaneously, sending the aircraft off the end of the flight deck at 165 miles an hour in two seconds. The activity is so intense that every effort is made to ensure a crew member is not blown over the side of the ship or sucked into the engine. The flight deck remains the most dangerous work stations anywhere.

The bridge is the control center of the ship's operations and is found on the starboard side of the deck. Looking forward starboard is the right side of the ship and port is the left side of the ship. The bridge has several decks that house the officers controlling the ship. Generally, the top deck is the Primary Flight Control sector. Beneath that deck is the Bridge with responsibility for the ship and its operations. The third deck down is Flag Bridge used by an admiral when one is aboard.

In the lower decks, we find all the personnel, equipment and living areas that actually perform the functions that make the ship fully operational. The hanger bay is a storage place for aircraft, especially for those being repaired. An elevator is located outside the body of the ship and is large enough to carry aircraft from the hanger bay to the flight deck.

Installation of an Air-Conditioner

The thought of moving to warm weather was encouraging, even if the temperatures would reach into the nineties, it would be better than freezing in Philadelphia. Toward the end of our stay in Philadelphia, I met with two civilian supervisors to discuss the possibility of installing an air conditioner in my quarters. One of the supervisors went with me to my quarters and checked to see if there was a vent that could be used as an exhaust for an air conditioner. He found one that fit the bill. While there, I called his attention to an indented area on the bulkhead about three feet wide and twenty inches deep that served no useful purpose. I asked if it could be made into a closet. He said "No problem."

I went to a local store and purchased an air conditioner; took it back to the ship and the crew installed it. We turned it on and it worked perfectly. Before they left, I noticed the indent in the bulkhead had disappeared. The indent was now covered with a door that matched the bulkhead around it. It didn't look like a door. The supervisor showed me how to open it. It became a hidden treasure closet for storing anything I may not want out in the public

Repairs Completed We Returned To Mayport, Florida

After anchoring in Hampton Roads to take on ammo and fuel, we set sail for Mayport, Florida on May 26, 1966, arriving at our homeport on June 2. Returning to Mayport, Florida was well received by the crew, as it gave time off to be with their families while preparations for our shakedown cruise in Caribbean were being made. While at sea for any length of time, air operations were carried out giving the pilots opportunities to keep their flight and landing skills at a very high level.

After returning to Mayport, Florida, our home port, the *Shang* continued air operations off the coast of Northern Florida for several days which included a return to Norfolk Naval ship yards to replace four of the ships screws. While operating off the coast of Northern Florida, we had an "at sea funeral" fulfilling the wishes of Rear Admiral Charles Hastings who requested that he be buried at sea. This ceremony proved to be a lesson on end of life realities. His body was wrapped and carried on a stretcher by four sailors. When we reached the side of the ship, I offered some prayers and signaled to the crew that it was time to send his body to the deep. A few seconds later, the body was released and slid off the stretcher and disappeared under the waves immediately. I thought it was a fate that awaits all of us, hopefully leaving this world to a better place. As scheduled, we returned to Mayport and began preparing the ship to meet the supply needs of our Mediterranean tour. While anchored ashore, fuel supplies and ammunition supplies were loaded; and we were under way. While at sea, Commander Alfred Nemoff safely completed his one thousandth arrested carrier landing, becoming the second Naval pilot to reach that level. On September 23, Captain Strong took over the command of the Shangri-La and completed the remainder of the Mediterranean cruise preparations.

Caribbean Shakedown Cruise

Once we had a full complement of personnel, we prepared to leave the shipyard and began our shakedown cruise in the Caribbean near Guantanamo Bay. We left Mayport, Florida on June 20 and anchored off Gitmo on June 22 and began a five weeks refresher training program. When we reached the Caribbean, we encountered a severe change in weather. The outside temperature was hot. The sun bearing down on the steel hull made working on the flight deck more difficult than usual. However, while the ship was underway, a breeze would somewhat temper the heat. I believe sunbathing was prohibited. To do so would give a severe burn in a very short time. Once, the ship's air conditioning system failed, giving the ship's interior the atmosphere of an oven. This problem was corrected and eventually cool air began to reach most parts of the ship making the rest of the cruise rather comfortable.

As an aside, while we were anchored in Guantanamo, we remained aware we were not in friendly waters. This called for maintaining a constant vigilance to prevent damage to our ship. As a safety precaution, whenever the watch saw bubbles approaching the ship, hand grenades were dropped on the bubbles to prevent any Cuban divers from reaching the ship and attaching explosives to the ship's hull. Additionally, our demolition divers would search the hull of the ship regularly looking for explosives that could cause some serious damage to the hull of the ship and inflict harm on equipment and personnel.

Several Days in Jamaica

Our training programs were intense, demanding a great deal of all hands. On July 15th, the crew received a break. We sailed to Jamaica for some R & R. The weather was perfect with more than ample opportunities to enjoy a few days' vacation. I spent time walking around the business area, and eventually made some inquiries concerning the possibility of a Catholic school on the island. I discovered there was a primary grade school so I took the opportunity to meet the staff and students. I made a practice of doing this in most of the countries we visited. Some characteristics were common to all of them; nuns taught the classes, the children wore uniforms, classes were disciplined and the students were busy studying.

This island has a large active military population and a considerable number of retired military personnel. However, the native population had many characteristics identifying them as former British subjects. The most obvious of which was the manner of speaking English. They had a British accent indicating, in the past, the island had been governed by the British.

One custom visitors to the island found interesting was the manner in which its traffic control officers managed traffic through crowded intersections. The officer stood on a small platform in the center intersection directing traffic. Their uniform included a white hat, jacket and gloves making it impossible not to see them. Several gave traffic signals with choreographic displays turning the signal into a work of art. Visitors, like me, would stop and watch the display for a few moments before moving on.

Return to Gitmo and Refresher Training

When we returned to Cuban waters, we were able to take advantage of some shore leave to visit the Guantanamo Naval Base. On a few occasions, I went ashore to visit and have dinner with the chaplain Benny Walker. As rotations in our duty stations moved us to various naval or Marine bases, we met again in Pensacola, Florida where we each had a two year assignment. When we had completed our shakedown cruise, our schedule called for an "Operational Readiness Inspection." The ship received a satisfactory rating. This level of rating did not sit well with our skipper because the inspection did not take into account the fact we had a green crew onboard lacking the decision competence ordinarily onboard our ship. While the ship was undergoing repairs in Philadelphia, the crew was transferred to other ships where their skills were needed. So, when the repairs were completed, we took on a new crew that had little experience on the work they were assigned to perform and for the most part had never been to sea. The crew needed a large learning curve which they received. However, this was not taken into account during the Readiness Inspection.

In prior years, the island was a much desired retirement billet for senior officers allowing them to spend their Twilight Cruise, their last cruise managing this base. An interesting event took place while we were in Cuban waters. A Russian-built transport aircraft flew over the ship and then flew northeast out of the area where we were operating. It seemed they were sending us a message –you're not alone nor perfectly safe.

Fresh Water Supplies Problem

A problem that happened several times on the *Shangri-La* and on other carriers of like size and age was a shortage of fresh water for drinking, bathing, air conditioning and for use by the catapults. The fresh water system on this class carrier was not originally designed to convert the amount of fresh water needed for operating a carrier with a catapult. Although the addition of the catapult system stressed the equipment, the ship managed to convert a sufficient amount of fresh water for our operational needs. However, we had a short period when fresh water supplies did not meet all the ship's needs resulting in creating a shortage of water for showers. At times like this, "Sailor showers" prove useful – wet down, turn off the water, soap up and then turn the water back on and rinse off. This problem was an occasional source of concern throughout its operations. On one occasion, a leak in the fresh water tanks was discovered. The necessary repairs were completed, bringing our water levels up to normal.

The readiness exercises were completed on July 15 and we returned to Mayport, arriving on July 28, 1966.

Chapter 17
Mediterranean Cruise and Meeting Pope Pius VI

On September 29, 1966, we left the Mayport area and began our cruise to the Mediterranean. Once our ship got underway, Air Wing 10 assigned to the *Shang* began flying onboard. Aircraft included Crusaders and Skyhawks performing their required functions, some of which included Fighting Squadrons, Light Photo and anti-Submarines Squadrons. Just prior to entering the Mediterranean, seven destroyers and two Oilers joined our group, completing our composition of ships. Before entering the Mediterranean, we had flight operations off the coast of Rota, Spain.

As we entered the Mediterranean, we passed the Rock of Gibraltar. This historical island helped make the cruise an unforgettable experience and a great beginning to our seven month Mediterranean tour. Stars looked like points of light resting on a black velvet background. A warm breeze pushed lightly against us as we stood on the flight deck watching planes being moved into position for night operations. Characteristically, the roar of aircraft engines at full throttle combined with the hiss of steam from the catapults demanded wearing headgear or you would suffer damage to your hearing. During flight ops, the noise on the flight deck was so intense it would be fruitless to try to hold a conversation. However, flight training and showing the flag are the major reasons for our deployment to the Mediterranean and other destinations. During our cruise, the *Shangri-La* was alive with aircraft practicing day and night flight operations. On this particular evening, the sky was exceedingly dark making the flames from the jet engines look like an exploding furnace. To shove an airplane weighing 29,000 lbs. off the deck of an aircraft carrier requires a great force stressing the importance of a catapult to assist in the process. As each aircraft reaches altitude, they form a squadron and begin practicing combat maneuvers.

Flying combat missions, whether in practice or actually involved in warfare, is always filled with dangers. Some formations bring aircraft into close quarters with each other. Travelling at hundreds of miles an hour, a slight movement of the controls could rapidly place an aircraft in a position for a mid-air collision, destroying one or both of the aircraft and, at times, taking the life of one or both pilots. During one of our night training exercises, two of our aircraft had a mid-air collision. Both aircraft were severely damaged and lost but both pilots bailed out safely. They were picked up by one of our helicopters and returned to our ship. Neither pilot was injured although both were taken to sick bay for a medical examination in the event they had sustained an injury that required medical attention.

An Aircraft Landing on the Flight Deck Loses a Fuel Tank

Shortly after we arrived in the Med, on October 16, a Skyhawk was making a landing on the flight deck when one of its fuel tanks ruptured, spilling fuel over the landing area and caught fire. It took six minutes to put the fire out. In that short time, the recently installed aluminum panels buckled, leaving our aircraft unable to make any landings. The pilot escaped without serious injury. The damage was so extensive it was beyond the capability of the ship's crew to restore the flight deck. To have the necessary repairs, we sailed to Naples and employed Italian ship builders. Their competence level was acceptable but Italian customs brought about some new problems. US Naval regulations prohibit drinking alcohol on American ships. Italian custom insists shipbuilders and others onboard a ship be allowed to drink wine during their meals. Since wine and liquor, generally, not allowed on US Navy ships, a problem arose immediately. Eventually, a resolution was reached and the work of repairing the flight deck continued. A new problem occurred when stormy weather arose. An offer was made by our command to fly the work crews to the ship using our helicopters. But the workers refused to use the helicopters, further delaying the repair. Eventually, the *Shang* had the repairs completed and left port for the open seas where we resumed our flight exercises.

Given the nature of carrier operations, danger involving loss of life is of continuous concern. Although every effort is made to ensure the safety of all hands, accidents happen. An example is the death of a young lieutenant who, while conducting maneuvers, experienced problems with his aircraft. When it became impossible to continue his flight, he bailed out of the plane. During the process of exiting the plane, he was seriously injured and died from the injury. When the rescue crew arrived at the scene of the crash they found him face down in the water and returned him to the ship's hospital. I don't know the percentage of times bailing out resulted in this kind of accident but it must be miniscule. It does, however, happen. Another accident took place to a sailor working on the flight deck when a Crusader aircraft was being moved. He stepped behind a jet blast that blew him over the side and into a gun tub. He suffered severe head injuries and died within the hour. Given the dangerous nature of flight deck work, the need is great for constant vigilance and ongoing training programs to prevent such accidents from becoming a common occurrence.

Repairs in Naples, Italy with Extended Liberty Allowed the Crew

Repairing the flight deck kept us anchored off Naples for about seven weeks. Although it hindered our participation in NATO fleet exercises, it did afford the crew an opportunity to take advantage of more relaxed shore leave.

Colonel Pat Harrington and his wife were friends from my tour in Camp Pendleton. Pat arranged an opportunity for me to fly with a Marine Air Wing stationed in Alameda, California. To do so required a couple of training programs to be taken prior to making such a flight. At the time I was there, several other people were taking the same training programs. Some of them I still remember. In preparation for the air flight, I had to learn how to eject from the plane safely. The training took place at a field station and consisted of experiencing what it would feel like when someone had to bail out of the aircraft. The training consisted of sitting on an aircraft seat attached to a steel girder rising from the base of the girder to about ten feet in the air. The girder was set at about a ten degree angle. I was strapped into the seat and prepared to be shot up the girder. I had just settled in when an explosion sent me shooting up the top of the girder. My body was at the top of the girder but my thinking process was still at the bottom of the machine. I got off the seat fully aware that if the occasion arrived requiring me to bail out of an aircraft, the ejection mechanism would throw me a considerable distance from the aircraft hopefully followed by an open parachute. The other training event I remember took place when several of us entered into a room where we were to experience what happens to us when we encounter a loss of oxygen. We simulated flying into higher altitudes with the level of oxygen getting lower as we reached higher altitudes. The higher we went the amount of available oxygen decreased; a very uncomfortable experience.

Following the training, I received the traditional award, an "OH My ASS" certificate for having ridden the ejection seat. Sometime later, I dressed for the flight and mounted a jet aircraft. There were two jets in our group. Before starting our run down the airstrip the pilot said "In the event we have to bail out of the aircraft I will say 'Bailout' three times. The first time I say it you must bail out immediately because when I say it the third time, I will bailout." The possibility of bailing out left me quickly as we began to maneuver into various formations, chasing the other jet, using the clouds for cover and making turns that felt like we were pulling five Gs. It was a great experience and increased my respect for our pilots' physical and mental competence.

While in Naples, I visited Pat who was assigned to a Marine Command in Naples. I visited the family who gave me a tour of the ruins of Pompeii. This visit to Pompeii proved to be one of the highlights of my tour of the Mediterranean. We spent an afternoon learning about the city, its citizens and how the city was destroyed.

Visit to Pompeii and Mount Vesuvius

Pompeii was a thriving Roman city south of Naples, Italy. On August 24th, 79 AD, Mount Vesuvius, on the outskirts of the city, erupted so violently it blew off the top of the mountain sending it twelve miles into the sky at twice the speed of sound and pouring volcanic red hot rocks, ashes and pumice down the side of the volcano at seventy miles an hour, covering the city with twenty feet of volcanic debris. Over time, the volcanic ash became as hard as rock. Pompeii had a population of twenty thousand, most of who managed to escape. However, 2,000 citizens decided to ride it out and stayed in the city. The heat and deadly gas killed all of them. The heat reached a level of thirteen hundred degrees, so hot it sucked the moisture out of the bodies of those who remained. The city was lost but was rediscovered in the eighteenth century after being buried for some 1,748 years. When excavation started to reveal the remnants of this lost city, they discovered a well-appointed city with facilities and structures and buildings with amazing architecture. It had restaurants, bars, tourist facilities, water fountains, an amphitheater and bath houses. There were water fountains, sophisticated water supply systems, drainage and sewage disposal systems for both public and private use. Buildings were found with mosaics on its walls. It had commercial establishments and stone streets, making it superior to most other cities of that period of history. It was a favorite resort for wealthy Romans. This visit proved to be an extraordinary study of history and a moving experience to stand in a city as it was hundreds years ago. Those who chose not to leave the town, especially a woman holding her child, ended their lives in a matter of seconds when debris struck the city.

The advantage of being in Naples is this city is the third largest city in Italy with a history dating back to 200 BC. With a generous leave policy, we were able to travel within the city famous for its museums and religious structures, great restaurants and to spend time in a world immersed in the history of civilization. Dr. Jack Race, Fleet Surgeon and I made arrangements for a flight to the States for crew members travelling home for the Christmas holidays. The travel service selected had been used by ship crews for several years before our arrival in the Mediterranean. When the arrangements were complete, the director of company invited us to dinner at his home. The manner in which the meal was served surprised both of us. The meal began with servings of pasta and assorted vegetables, bread and an aged wine with a pleasant aroma and a smooth, pleasing texture. Believing this was to be the main course, we ate accordingly. Just when we thought the meal was completed, the main course arrived featuring a roast, sausages and other items brought to the table. The fragrance of the roast and sausages filled the room. We took portions of everything, hoping our stomachs would hold the volume of food we had consumed. Then the meal ended with a salad, unlike the cakes, pies and ice cream generally ending our meals. We returned to the ship fully aware of the reason Naples is so famous for the meals served throughout the city. The next day, we met with the KLM airlines representative who made all the arrangements for the holiday flight.

Trip to Rome

Naples has a high speed rail service to various cities in Italy. Several of us decided to use this service for a trip to Rome where we could explore some of its historical sites. One of our primary objectives was to spend some time at Vatican City, the home of St. Peter's Basilica. Eight of us made the trip and spent our time visiting sites for which the city is famous, like the Coliseum, a structure that has survived nearly two thousand years. The structure was constructed over a period of ten years from 70AD to 80AD. Although a part of its wall is missing, there is no doubt the structure is an engineering marvel. In recognition of this feat, it is one of the Seven New Wonders of the World. We visited the Parthenon and the Roman Forum and found the Trevi Fountain most interesting. All of the sites reminded us of the tremendous impact the Roman Empire had on the civilized world.

We spent time visiting as many places as we could reach with the time limits. One of them I clearly remember. There was a saying "if you sit outside a restaurant on the Via Veneto Street in Rome, after a few hours you will have seen some of the world's most important and internationally known people." Being anxious to test the saying, we decided to have lunch at one of the restaurants, sat outside the building and examined the people passing by trying to identify these very important people. We sat there for about an hour or so having lunch and studying the passersby. Finally it dawned on us; if the rich and famous did pass us we probably would not know any of them. However, it was not a total loss. We did see dozens of the "hoi polloi" hurrying past us and a few others who took tables like we did looking for the rich and famous who probably would not walk down the Via

Veneto and be watched by complete strangers. If they had any sense, they would take a vehicle and avoid the curious altogether.

St. Peter's Basilica, Rome and visit with Pope Paul VI

Later in the day, we entered the Piazza San Pietro and found ourselves overwhelmed by the size and beauty of the Piazza and the order of the atrium resembling outstretched arms reaching out from St. Peter's Basilica seeming to embrace those in the Piazza and probably the world generally. As we drew near the Basilica, we found the size of the building breathtaking. The doors guarding the entrance were huge, strong, appearing to be rugged enough to withstand an army of unwanted forces. Its reputation of being one of the largest churches in the world was well deserved. Once we entered, we found ourselves enveloped in a world where the worship of God dominated everything: the altars, shrines, and numerous artifacts called attention to it being the House of God. Silence permeated the atmosphere, making the sound of our whispers much louder than they actually were. A few minutes into the church, we knew how important it would be to have a guide to identify the work of the many great artists who decorated the Basilica. However, even without a guide we explored as much of the building as time allowed. Eventually, we arrived at the altar, the central feature of the Basilica, famous for its design - especially the construction of the dome that covered such a large area. The bronze columns supporting the bronze canopy over the altar held our attention; the weight and design of the materials made us aware of the genius required to design and build such a magnificent structure. It was spectacular and the center of our attention.

Visiting St. Peter's tomb was an incredible experience. To be able to stand in the presence of the first of the apostles, knowing two thousand years earlier he went about introducing Jesus to the then-known world and remembering he died trying; to be in the presence of this saint surrounded by the history of Christianity reminded us of the indispensable role he played in building the foundations of our faith; a true "sine qua non." The genius of Michael Angelo and others who contributed their great talent to the development of this basilica were visible everywhere. As we approached the altar, we saw four of the spiral formed bronze columns up close. We learned the columns stood one hundred feet above the altar and supported a ninety three ton canopy, also made of bronze. Below the altar was the tomb of St. Peter the Apostle. Being aware some claim this location may not be the tomb of St. Peter, those of us who stood there had no doubt of its authenticity. Recently, Pope Francis presented the bones of St. Peter to the thousands of faithful standing in the court yard beneath the balcony at the close of the Year of Faith ceremony.

Moving around the Basilica, we discovered a stairwell leading to the ceiling of the Basilica often used by visitors to St. Peters. We were all in good shape so we climbed to the top onto a platform which gave us a view of Rome and the countless structures displaying the city's long history. One thing captured our attention. On top of one of the buildings was a big Coca Cola sign; at first we were surprised but with a little thought we realized Coca Cola is now found worldwide.

When we returned to the main body of the church, a priest saw us in our US Naval uniforms. He asked if we would like to be in an audience with the Holy Father, Pope Paul V1. We said we would be honored and he led us to a private room where perhaps fifteen dignitaries dressed in formal attire were waiting to meet the pope. Women, in formal black dresses nearly touching the floor, had their heads covered by black silk scarves. The men in formal dress formed a line across the width of the room. We stood several feet behind them. Pope Paul VI entered the room greeting each visitor personally in their respective languages. We discovered later the Pope was fluent in twelve languages. As he reached the end of the line, he glanced up and saw us, American sailors in uniform standing toward the back of the room. He stopped, looked at us, smiled and waved his hand and gave us his blessing. We felt honored he gave us a special recognition and his blessing. We discussed the correctness of St. Peter's tomb being located here serving as an anchor for all of us who came to know Christ because of his efforts. Having completed our tour of Rome, we returned to the railroad depot bringing with us a host of memories of Rome, St Peter's Basilica and the many other wonders that filled our visit.

Trip to Our Lady of Lourdes Shrine in Lourdes France

During our Mediterranean tour, many of us were aware we were close to Lourdes, a town in Southern France. Since 1879, hundreds of miracles have been credited to this Shrine and as evidenced by the countless crutches, canes, and other assistive medical articles left there by people who had received a cure during their visit. A number of us took advantage of our location Naples, and made a trip to the Shrine. Together, we planned a trip on a sleeper train that took us directly to Lourdes. I don't remember much about the train ride except I fell asleep for the full ride. I did find it comfortable, despite the cold winter conditions and the clicking noise the train made as it passed over the separations in the tracks. We were anxious to see the pile of crutches, wheel chairs and other aids left by the disabled who visited the Shrine and received the cure they requested. When they were cured, many of them left their mobility supports at the Shrine as a demonstration of the cure they had received. We arrived, found a taxi and made our way to the Shrine. The town was small, about fifteen thousand people which surprised all of us.

Part of the tour of the Shrine was to bathe in the water flowing from the Shrine of the Blessed Mother. To accommodate visitors wanting to bathe in the waters at the Shrine, there were a number of screened-in structures at the end where small private cubicles were located. We could change clothes into a loin cloth and bathe in the tubs three quarters full of water. The process involved entering the tub and submerging in the water for a short period, during which a prayer is offered and a favor of our Blessed Mother requested. At each tub there was an assistant who met us and took us to the tubs, showed us where we could change in privacy and helped us get into the tub. It was really cold out so, when I got to the tub, I stood at the end hesitant to enter the cold water. I turned around to the attendant and commented on the temperature of the water. Then he immediately came to my assistance. He gave me a push and within seconds I was in the tub, fully covered with really freezing water. I got out of the tub faster than I got into it. Actually I got out so fast I don't recall saying a single prayer or asking for a favor. As I was drying, I looked at the helper who smiled and asked "That wasn't all that bad was it?" I agreed, dressed quickly and met with the rest of our group. We were happy to have had the opportunity to visit the Shrine of the Blessed Mother and witness the many expressions of faith found in the pile of discarded medical equipment. We spent several hours in the town, had breakfast and made our way back to the train. Most of us never thought we would have an opportunity to visit Lourdes. Taking advantage of this opportunity gave us a confirmation that prayers are answered, making the impossible possible.

Palma Mallorca (Diamond of the Mediterranean)

While at sea in the Mediterranean, we had liberty at some of the port cities. Larger ships like a carrier would normally anchor at ports with large populations. When this happened, I would visit a parish with a school to tell the students something about the USA and discuss the operations of a ship as large as an aircraft carrier. When we set anchor at Palma Mallorca, an island 132 miles off the coast of Spain known as the "Diamond of the Med," I was able to visit the Bishop of Palma Mallorca and introduce our crew as visitors to this very famous island. To set up a visit with the Bishop, I went to one of the local parishes to find a priest who could speak English. I found one when I made the first contact. He went with me to meet the Bishop and acted as an interpreter. The Bishop recognized my French name saying it was a Normandy name and it is possibly the district from which my ancestors had migrated to Canada and eventually to the USA. He welcomed our crew and said he hoped the sailors would enjoy their stay on the island. He recommended a trip around the island to see some of their beautiful beaches and for those who played golf to find some excellent courses. We spent about a half hour with the Bishop.

On our way back to the parish rectory, I asked the priest if the parish had a school. He said the parish did have a primary grade school with classes through the eighth grade. He invited me to visit the school. I did and appreciated the warm welcome I received. To my surprise, the students had some knowledge of English but needed the sister to interpret some of my comments. I told them the carrier is a war ship built as an ocean going airport that allows aircraft to operate effectively in almost any region of the world. I told them our pilots conducted combat training exercises to keep their skills at a high level. They found it interesting how this ship was like a floating city; with stores, sleeping quarters, showers, mess halls (cafeterias) machine shop, movies, a hospital and a chapel where the Mass and other religious services could be held twenty-four hours a day. The students asked a lot of questions, most of which could be answered by a visit to the ship. So I asked them if they would like to go aboard the ship. All their hands went up at once, giving an enthusiastic yes. A nun sitting with us in the class room said she thought it could be done. I asked sister to have the students at the dock at 9:00 am the next morning and we would take them aboard the ship.

The next morning, with a clear sky and calm sea, the boatswain and I went to the dock and found the children already there, filled with excitement, waiting to go board the ship. We gave them a few safety precautions then loaded them onto the liberty boat and took them to the "*Shang.*" As we drew close to the ship, you could feel their excitement build. Pilots and some of the ship's crew were waiting for them. The flight deck had numerous aircraft with pilots at stand-by near each of them. The kids, bursting with anticipation, ran to the planes anxious to see them up close. During the visit, they were taken to every area they were allowed to see. A great thrill came when they sat in the airplanes, touched some of the controls and received a short discussion on the many gages and control instruments used to fly the aircraft. Their interest in the aircraft and all the instruments needed to launch one absorbed their attention. Their ability to speak and understand some English allowed them to ask questions of the pilots and crew and understand the responses. When everyone had taken advantage of a close-up look at the flight deck, sit in a fighter jet aircraft and examine the catapult system and huge elevator used for moving aircraft to and from the flight deck, the next step was a visit to the hanger bay where planes were being repaired and updated. Dozens of sailors were pouring over the aircraft, making sure they were ready and safe for flight. The size of the hanger bay is enormous and the equipment used to work on the aircraft could be dangerous making it unsafe for children to be up close to the repair activity. One of the officers gave them a short briefing about the activity carried on in the hanger bay. When this discussion was completed, our visitors were taken to the ship's mess hall where they were given a treat of milk, cookies and ice cream. Once they had finished eating, we completed a head-count to be sure we were taking back the same number of children we brought onboard a few hours earlier. We took them back to the liberty boat, helped them get onboard and returned them to the dock where the nuns were waiting for them. It was a great experience for the children and they expressed their thanks many times and told us our sailors were terrific. They truly enjoyed the visit to the *Shangri-La* and we enjoyed having them with us.

An unexpected benefit of having the young children onboard the *Shangri-La* was the enjoyment the crew experienced having children with them for a few hours, showing them around and answering their questions. Everyone in the ship's crew was eighteen years old or older. Having children around, hearing the sound of their innocent laugher and their intense curiosity about everything in and on the ship, proved to be a rewarding experience for our troops: an occasion they will long remember. The children understood they had just experienced an activity few if any other people in the world would ever be able to share.

A few days later, on Palm Sunday, sisters from the school prepared a beautifully decorated palm and brought it to the pier where they asked the boatswain to deliver it to me. The palm was a work of art and we used them for our Palm Sunday Mass.

Distressed Aircraft Crashed During Night Operations

Like all naval ships, the carrier must be in a constant state of readiness. Ship maintenance and aircraft receive constant attention. Problems can develop and when discovered, immediate action is taken to remedy the problem. Delays could be devastating. Military personnel are aware of their responsibilities and ensure their services will be on station when called. To stay in a state of readiness, pilots are constantly being trained in landing and take-off procedures as well as combat maneuvers involving individual and squadron training. This training involves day and night operations. No matter how well supervised, mistakes happen during updating procedures performed in the hanger bay. Watching an aircraft carrier in operation you become aware quickly of the countless dangers to which the pilots and crew are subjected every day. Dangers for pilots are not restricted to combat. On this specific night, a squadron flew off the flight deck to practice night maneuvers. The sky seemed blacker than usual, making the Mediterranean uninviting. The flight deck was alive with crew members preparing planes for takeoff and assisting aircraft returning from their maneuvers. Watching from the sidelines, I saw planes hooked to the catapult and subsequently shot off the deck. A burst of steam from the catapult with the full thrust of the aircraft's engine sent an F-18 fighter jet screaming down the flight deck reaching 165 miles an hour in two seconds. The pilot's body is pushed back into his seat leaving him fully aware that for a short period of time he has little or no control over his aircraft. As they leave the ship, some planes dip a bit and then roar up at rapidly at increasing speeds. As others joined around him, they formed a squadron and began carrying out their night training exercises.

Ten minutes later, command was notified someone in the squadron had a problem, his fuselage was on fire consuming the aircraft. He began descending rapidly toward an unfriendly ocean. Don and members of his squadron were screaming at him "Jack, bailout, your fuselage is on fire...Bailout now!!" The Mediterranean Sea at night is dark and foreboding. The speed at which the plane was falling left the pilot only a few seconds to eject safely from certain disaster. He heard the squadron yelling at him to eject. His controls stopped working as the aircraft plunged toward the sea. Jack hesitated to bail out. He did eject but not soon enough for the parachute to open and pull him away from the aircraft and avoid the crash. The squadron circled around his location, waiting for a rescue unit to arrive. A helicopter was sent to the scene hoping the pilot would still be alive. They found Jack in the wreckage, his parachute covering some of his body. They removed him from the wreckage and his remains were brought back to the ship.

When an accident like this happens, a number of actions must take place. The most important of which is to notify his wife and family. I received a call from the XO telling me to meet him at the ship's hospital. When I arrived, I was told his wife Jan had an apartment in

Taranto, Italy. As the Casualty Assistance Officer (CACO) I would be the one to notify her and offer assistance in getting the family and their house goods transferred back to the States. An airplane known as the COD (Carrier Onboard Delivery) was assigned to take me to the Naval Station in Taranto, Italy The base made a vehicle and driver available to drive me to her apartment. Notifying a family of the death of one of their family member is always difficult. It is so much greater when he is in his twenties, newly married, with his wife overseas. There were other wives there but it is not the same as having an immediate family member close at hand to share her grief. As the CACO officer, I had to make sure his wife was appropriately notified and arrangements made to bring her and her belongings back to the States. At the time, it seemed as if there were a thousand things requiring her attention including the selection of a burial site, a decision unthinkable until now. I met with the naval personnel stationed in Taranto to discuss the arrangement for Jan's return to the States. I was assured they had considerable experience in managing situations like this and that they were already taking the steps necessary to assist Jan. They assured us everything would be carried out appropriately and professionally.

Of all the things a chaplain has to do, delivering a death message to a husband or wife is absolutely the most difficult task. There are times when an experience like this will remain with you forever. This was such a case.

By the time I arrived at her apartment, it was well into the night and I could see there were no lights on in her apartment. Knowing this would be the last good night's rest she would get for a long time, I decided not to wake her up but to wait until I saw some lights go on indicating she was awake and probably making coffee. However, it was important to bring her this news early in the morning before wives of the other pilots would find out about the accident and start calling her to express their sorrow and arrange to go to her apartment to be with her and assist in any way they could. At 6:30 am, I saw the kitchen light go on and presumed she was up getting ready to begin her day. Her apartment was on the second floor. When I reached her apartment, I knocked on the door. As she opened it I saw a smile on her face and she said "good morning, Father." Then, in seconds, she realized this was not a social call. Something terrible had happened to Jack! Her smile faded; she turned ashen as she realized Jack had been seriously injured or killed. She slumped back into a kitchen chair, burst into tears saying "No! Dear God, no" I waited a minute or so before discussing an incident no wife ever wants to hear. All the wives of the pilots knew the dangers faced by the Navy pilot on active duty and were aware some could result in serious harm and even death. There is just no easy way to notify a wife her husband was killed in an accident. The news of the accident and the finality it brought to her was so devastating you could see her world crumbling around her. Her world seemed to come to an end. But life does not allow for long recovery periods. Almost immediately, her full attention will be called on as she responds to the many details required in making preparation for the interment of her husband and her return to the States. There will be difficult times, but this sense of loss will decrease as numerous actions call for her immediate attention. She will have to contact Jack's parents, as well as her own, determine where and what funeral services will be held; what actions to take as they too will have suggestions and concerns about funeral services and burial arrangements, and myriad other actions calling for her time and attention. Just as I had expected, shortly after my arrival at her apartment, her phone started to ring. Other wives living in the area began calling to express their sorrow and to volunteer to assist. Others did not wait to call. They hurried to her apartment ready to assist her to manage the news of her husband's death. By this time, I had completed my efforts. I told her the Navy would be contacting her immediately to assist her in taking all the actions required to move Jack's body to a location she wished and they would ensure her household goods would be handled carefully and shipped back to the states. I left promising to keep her in my prayers. I returned to the vehicle and drove back to the airport; thanked the staff for their assistance and made a call to the carrier to send a COD to pick me up and return me to the ship.

Helicopter Trips

Helicopters are complex aircraft equipped with assets that make them an extraordinary value to the service. Their use in the military has proven to be unmatched for their power and maneuverability. In civilian life, especially in the construction trade, they are recognized as workhorses that can move product and/or people unencumbered by stop lights, busy highways, etc. The helicopter has proven its worth as a transportation system by hospitals, construction and law enforcement but especially so in the military. At sea, it's a major convenience for transferring people and products from ship to ship or ship to shore in an efficient manner. When a pilot has to bail out of an airplane at sea, it is the helicopter that picks him up and returns him to the ship. The role it takes in combat is extraordinary as it can move close to a conflict; participate in the exchange of firepower with a .50 BMG round capable of delivering accurate shot placements at ranges over one thousand yards.

An example of their utility at sea took place while we were underway in the Mediterranean. A destroyer requested a visit by the Fleet Catholic Chaplain to offer Mass for his crew. The request was accepted and I was notified to make the necessary arrangements. We selected a day and time for the flight. Given the time for air ops, we determined early afternoon to be most appropriate. When I reached the helicopter the crew had already made the pre-flight safety check-up. I had prepared my Mass kit and arrived at the helicopter ready for the ride to the destroyer. I joined the flight crew as they were finalizing preflight preparations.

This was first time I used the helicopter while serving on the *Shangri-La*. While we made ready for the trip, the flight crew briefed me on how the aircraft would lower me to the deck of the destroyer and how I should wear the equipment needed during my trip down to the ship. If the ship had room on the main deck to accommodate a helicopter, the aircraft would land on the ship and disembark the passenger and his luggage. However, this ship had no landing space appropriate for a helicopter landing. The second option was to use a ring buoy to lower a passenger to the main deck of the ship. I would have to be lowered by holding on to a ring buoy ("donut dolly"). We climbed into the helicopter and I was given brief instructions on how to wear the buoy which consisted of putting my head, arms and shoulders through the hole in the ring, place the buoy under my arms and hang in this position until my feet touched the destroyer's deck. I was assured the system was absolutely safe. The buoy looked like a large donut attached to a cable. I put on the buoy, stepped to the entrance, sat down and slid off the deck. Immediately I felt the weight of my body pull me down into the buoy. I turned to the crew and signaled I'm ready for the trip. Then I looked down to see the destroyer. The ship's captain and two sailors were standing on the deck waiting for me. Looking down at the ship, it appeared to be at least several hundred feet or so below me. We hovered over the ship until the crew believed I could be lowered safely. They gave me a signal I was about to start down. I do not recall the height we were at when I slid out of the helicopter but I felt certain the skipper and crew on the ship had to be bigger than they looked like from this distance. Another reason for the height we had to fly was to avoid the super structures rising above the ship's main deck.

This ride was a whole new experience, hanging in a buoy a hundred plus feet above the ship's main deck. The pilot made sure we stayed away from the ship's superstructure. I remember hearing of a priest being lowered to the deck of a ship when a strong wind blew him against the ship's structure breaking several bones. I have no idea how the injured person could hold on with such severe pain, except he had no option. Regardless, our aircraft maintained a location directly over the main deck of the ship.

About a quarter of the way down, the cable slipped and I fell about ten feet or so and jerked to a stop leaving me a little concerned. This was followed by a period of a few seconds before the cable started down again. Shortly after the first stop, the pulley began operating properly. The cable began to lower me smoothly. Then after, several seconds, the cable problem reappeared and I had a free fall for another ten or twenty feet ending with a sudden stop. At this point I determined the crew was trying to scare me but there was no way I would show any signs of fear or concern. I determined not to let their mind games get to me. The rest of the ride was smooth all the way to the main deck. Once on deck, I got out of the harness and waited for my Mass kit to be lowered. I offered Mass in the evening, had dinner and went outside to experience being close to the water. While on the carrier, the only time I got close to the water was when I would take a liberty boat to go ashore. As I stood there, the sea began to change. The waves grew much higher and the ship reacted to the change making it less likely I would be returned to the carrier any time soon. A notice to our skipper confirmed our suspicion. I was given the XO's bunk for the night and, the next morning, I was picked up and returned to the carrier. While on the destroyer, it was great to feel the rise and fall of a smaller ship as we reacted more intimately with the waves. Although the carrier does react somewhat to the ocean's surface, it is far less reactive to a rough sea than is a destroyer, a much smaller ship. The following day, the helicopter picked me up and I returned to the *Shangri-La*.

After returning to the carrier, I made no comment to the helicopter crew about the cable problems. I thanked them for the ride, returned to my quarters and resumed my work schedule. I did not receive a reason for the cable problem until the last day onboard the *Shangri-La*. The crew came together to explained why the cable control system malfunctioned, slipping out of control twice on that ride down to the destroyer. I asked: "Knowing the problem, why didn't you move the plane away from the ship so if the pulley failed completely I would have been over the water with a chance of surviving the fall?" The answer was not encouraging. "If you were to fall to the surface of the ocean from the height we were at when the problem developed, hitting the water would have been as damaging as if you hit the steel deck. We did not tell you the real reason for the two slippages so you would not worry about taking rides in the future." Their reasoning was accurate. In future rides I would be a little concerned but take the rides aware sometimes machines malfunction. I was just happy my ride ended smoothly.

Man Overboard

A constant concern when flight operations are underway is the ever present danger of a sailor falling off the carrier's flight deck. The action during flight operations demands such intense concentration on the job at hand that accidents do happen. Someone on the flight deck would move to avoid an airplane being relocated or involved in some other actions placing him close to a side of the deck and not thinking of his location backs up and falls over the side. Given his job, he would be wearing a safety vest to keep him afloat until help arrives. Immediately, the loud speaker announces "Man overboard!" As is obvious by the size of the ship, it cannot stop immediately and pick him up. The procedure used in cases like this is the ship goes into a formation resembling the figure "8" while it is slowing down. When the form "8" is completed, the ship will be back at the site where the sailor went overboard and is waiting to be picked up. Given the size of an aircraft carrier and the fact that it has helicopters onboard, this maneuver is not required. During air ops, there was always a helicopter operating near the ship in the event it is needed for such emergencies.

Of course, falling overboard is not restricted to the crew on the flight deck, it can happen to other members of the crew, like me. While ashore I had purchased a mink shawl for my mother and had it wrapped for shipment to the US. The package was actually water proof. On a cloudy mid-morning day, we were anchored off the coast of Spain in the Mediterranean. A friend on another ship with orders to return to the US offered to take it with him and overnight it to my mom when the ship reached stateside. My intention was to leave the "*Shang*" on a liberty boat to bring the package to him. On this occasion, the waves on the Med were higher than usual causing the liberty boat to rise and fall about four feet.

The boarding process involved waiting until the liberty boat rises to the level of the platform at the end of the ladder, then step off the platform into the boat for a ride to the dock where I would give him the package for shipment to my parent's home. I watched the waves move the liberty boat to the height of the ladder platform and then sink about four feet. A few seconds later, it rose to an appropriate height for boarding. This time, I watched the waves start upward to the platform. I heard what I thought was the liberty boat hitting the platform. Presuming the boat was next to the platform, I stepped off without bothering to take a second look. I stepped off the ladder and, looking up, I saw no boat, lots of ocean and the space between us rapidly closing. To my complete surprise the boat was not there and I was rushing into the water. I was too far away to step back to the platform. I tried to hold on to the box but, when I hit the water the box was pushed out of my arms and started floating away from the ship. In one of our conferences, we were told if this did happen, to avoid being cut to pieces by the liberty boat propellers, dive and allow the boat to move away from the platform. So, I dove immediately and kept going deeper until realized I was at the keel of the ship and needed a rapid move upward before I ran out of air. I turned my direction and started swimming upward. As I broke the surface, I took a huge breath of air and noticed an officer on the platform removing his shoes preparing to come in after me. He looked relieved to see me surface. I climbed back onto the platform and made my way back to the hanger bay.

My package was now floating about thirty yards from me. I yelled at the boatswain to pick up my package. He waved letting me know he heard my request. As I started to climb back up the ladder making my way to the hanger bay, I heard over the loudspeaker "Man overboard!" My clothes were dripping wet and my shoes felt like the bottom of a swimming pool. In the meantime, a light rain had started to fall. I climbed back up the ladder and, upon reaching the hanger bay, I met two sailors who were about to leave the ship to go ashore. One of them asked if it was raining. Answering, I said "Raining? Look at me!" Everything from head to toe was sopping wet, water dripping off my coat running down my sleeves. I looked like I had been swimming fully dressed and, of course, I had. They turned around and went back probably to get rain coats. My clothing, including my shoes, did eventually dry up but it took a bit longer to recover my pride. Needless to say, I took greater care when I made future transfers to the liberty boats.

Navy Relief Fund

The Navy Relief Fund plays an important role assisting sailors, Marines and their families in difficult times. Most often this meant giving them money to take care of unexpected expense or helping out with other problems involving their family members. Each year, all Navy and Marine installations hold a Navy Relief Fund Drive. To make the drive more effective on our ship, the skipper authorized having a raffle in which the winner would receive a week's vacation in the USA at no travel costs during the Christmas holidays. To ensure no one would be offended by participating in the lottery, the Captain called both chaplains to discuss the issue. We assured him the practice was for a good cause and should not offend any one's religious principles. Those who may have a problem with gambling could give a donation directly to the fund without participating in the raffle.

Managing the fund drive was given to the ship's surgeon, Jack Race, and me. We did extensive recruitment among the crew. Having the Christmas week at home made contributing very attractive. We had already spent several months away from home so a trip back to the states to be with their families during this important holiday proved to be a major selling point. Everyone was extremely generous and, of course, hopeful that they would win. The drive ended with a program in the hangar bay where a winner was to be randomly selected by a crew member. We made the selection process an entertaining occasion and decided to select the newest member of our crew to reach into the box and pull out the name of the winner.

The seaman selected arrived onboard the *Shang* two days before the drawing. He walked to the table, reached in and pulled out a ticket, looked at the name, immediately he had a very concerned look on his face. Apologetically, he handed me the ticket. Looking out at thousands of anxious faces, I read the name aloud and waited for someone to raise their hand but no one did. Then I heard a soft voice whisper, "Father, that's me." The new seaman picked his own name. In total disbelief, I turned around to face him saying "this cannot happen." He just came on board. He looked at me and tried to smile but his demeanor told me he was far from being a happy camper. Obviously, he realized that this was not really fair to the men who had been at sea for months. When I read his name out loud and he raised his hand an overwhelming moan came from the thousands of troops realizing that he had just come onboard two days earlier. Fortunately, the skipper and XO were at the drawing. We had a brief discussion and the skipper decided to have a second drawing. This one went to a crew member with a lot of time onboard. Both of them were given tickets for their flights home. I don't recall the amount of money put into the Navy Relief Fund but it was substantial.

Chapter 18
Assignment to Ellyson Field Naval Air Station Pensacola Florida

W hen my tour on the *Shangri-La* came to an end, I received orders to Ellyson Field Naval Air Station, Pensacola, Florida. As usual, I asked the Air Force for a ride back to the states. They had a refueling tanker making the trip, so I joined the tanker crew as a "spare boom operator." I had observed this style aircraft from a distance but never up close. The Boeing KC-135 Stratotanker is a massive aircraft weighing around 322,500 lbs. When fully loaded, the aircraft carries about 225,000 pounds of transferable fuel. Among military aircraft, the KC-135 resembles an aircraft carrier in comparison with other military combat aircraft.

As we started down the runway, we knew at once we were not flying a fighter jet or a commercial aircraft. It reminded me of a giant albatross working to get its huge body off the water's surface and into the air. I watched the second hand on my watch but changed to looking at the minute hand as we were gaining speed moving down the air strip. After several minutes, the plane would rise off the runway and settle back down trying to become airborne. Another passenger, an Air Force pilot, looked at me and said "Don't sweat it. It takes a long time for this monster to get airborne. It'll get there." I am not sure about the speed the tanker would require to take off but I do know that the aircraft travelled a long way down the airstrip before we were in-flight. I am told that the airstrips used for this aircraft are five miles long. Our take off effort certainly proved that the airstrip should be at least five miles long or longer.

The trip proved to be an extraordinary experience. On our flight back to the states we flew over the USS *Shangri-La*. It looked about the size of a postage stamp. The pilot of our craft commented that he would never want to land an airplane on a carrier. Having spent two years on the carrier, I had to agree with him; there were definite dangers associated with aircraft landing on a restricted landing space at a speed of 145 miles per hour. Navy pilots are extraordinary people. Landing a fighter aircraft at that speed on less than five hundred feet of deck space, could have some really consequential difficulties. Should you miss one of the restraining wires you get the chance to do it all over again. It takes more brains and guts than most people could muster. Seeing the carrier brought back a lot of wonderful memories. Serving on the *"Shang"* proved to be some of the greatest years of my life.

Ellyson Field, Naval Helicopter Training Center

Being transferred to Pensacola, the home of Naval Aviation, promised to be an interesting tour. Pensacola had a huge military population composed primarily of Navy aircraft related operations. Mainside was the major Naval Station in the Pensacola complex and had the largest number of employees in the counties of Escambia and Santa Rosa, Florida. It employed sixteen thousand military and seventy-four hundred civilian personnel. The base is best known as a Naval Air Schools Command where students receive technical training and the Marines participate in training support groups. This is also home to the Blue Angels Navy Flight Demonstration Squadron. This part of Florida had several naval air stations, and a huge naval aircraft repair facility on Mainside employing hundreds of federal employees. Mainside has two major roads leading onto the base. The most trafficked one is the road from the city of Pensacola. Every day of the work week, thousands of military and civilian personnel use this road to enter the base. For about a two hour time frame, the traffic moving on the boulevard onto the base made crossing the street to go in the opposite direction almost impossible. To make a left turn across two lanes of traffic would require the use of a hover craft. One of the chaplains, Don Mc Grogan, who lived just off Navy Blvd., would drive with base traffic through the Mainside base gate enter the base and drive around the guard shack and take Warrington RD out of the base to drive to his base.

Mainside, as it is referred to, is home to dozens of Naval and Marine training commands. Six thousand military and civilian personnel from 150 countries attend education training that include surface, subsurface and air training programs. Students training through programs offered at this command are able to earn Associates, Bachelors and Masters Degrees. It has an 18 hole golf course and a three par course. Several of us met almost weekly to play golf on one or the other of the courses. It has a Naval Air Museum with so many artifacts it could easily burn up several hours of your time viewing this extraordinary history of naval air. Actually, it had all the characteristics of a good sized city, including a base hospital, and Sherman Air Field that daily handled a considerable amount of aircraft.

Ellyson Field was the Naval Helicopter Training Center. The importance of the base training programs was demonstrated throughout the Vietnam era and continued for years following this conflict. Pilots trained to fly helicopters during the Vietnam war became the life blood of the war carrying supplies and troops engaged in ground warfare. When I arrived at Ellyson Field and checked in with Headquarters, I was given authority to live off base. I contacted a realtor and worked with him to find a house I could afford. It took several days to find one in my price bracket. The house had to be big enough to accommodate visits by my parents and friends. A number of the priests from Upper Michigan came to spend a few days on the beach, play some golf and just enjoy the warm weather. Although this base no longer exists, during the Vietnam war, Ellyson Field was alive and a fully operational training facility for Navy, Marine, Coast Guard and some Air Force helicopter pilots. The Vietnam war was in full force and Ellyson trained thousands of helicopter pilots. In 1967, when I arrived at the base, we were graduating around twenty-five hundred pilots a year. The demand for their skills was constant and grew each year as the war continued. The number of Army and Navy/Marine helicopter pilots who served in Vietnam clearly shows the importance placed on the helicopters as an effective weapon. Forty thousand helicopter pilots served in Vietnam. Helicopters were the work horses of the Navy and Marine Corps. Given their unique design, this made them an excellent vehicle for operations involving the movement of material and men rapidly and efficiently as the needs of the service required. Their fire power was often used to participate in combat situations giving ground crews aerial assistance in removing enemy encampments. These, and other such engagements by the helicopters, continually placed them in the line of heavy enemy fire. Their rescue missions brought them into combat areas submitting them to enemy fire at very close range. I remember one of the helicopter pilots told us that he was flying General Nickerson over a combat area where the general was observing the conflict from above the fight zone and had the pilot hover over the fight zone while he called out directions to the Marines below, telling them where the enemy fire was coming from and how best to encounter the Vietnamese troops. He evaluated that experience as a life-changing event as he waited for enemy fire from below to blow them out of the sky. Of course, they both lived to tell about it. Many others were not so lucky. Thousands of our pilots and crew members lost their lives serving in Vietnam. One practice that helped save pilot lives was placing a bullet- proof vest on the seat of the aircraft since enemy fire often came from Vietnamese ground troops and the vest would afford some additional protection.

Being fully aware of the dangers soon to be faced by the new graduating pilots, the graduation ceremonies had a happy but somber side. Graduation ceremonies were held in the base chapel because of its appropriate setting and because it was large enough to hold the graduates and their families. All of them approached their new responsibilities with enthusiasm, anxious to become involved with their special skills.

On one occasion, an instructor at the base took the two of us chaplains for a helicopter ride and, when we landed, he told us we would each have a chance to take control of the plane and see if we could hold the aircraft steady while hovering over a piece of ground without moving it up or down or to either side. He reminded us that the aircraft could almost fly itself and that difficulties experienced by students involved unconsciously moving the stick with forward, backward or sideways pressure. Believing that he was putting zero pressure on the stick, suddenly the helicopter would start to move upward as he watched the earth slowly move away from him. Dick Delany, the base Protestant chaplain, was the first to try holding the aircraft steady with no movement. He did an excellent job. When I was given control of the aircraft, I discovered how reactive the aircraft was to any movement of the control stick. Like Dick, I held the stick steady without any movement. Even though we had absolutely no idea of how to fly a helicopter, he believed we would have passed the hover test.

As the classes passed through our training program, at the graduation ceremony our prayer was that each of them would serve the country courageously and return alive with memories of a job well done.

Our chapel was located just inside the main gate. On Sundays, some civilians would attend our 8:00 or 10:00 o'clock Mass. We were fortunate to have one of the civilians play the organ for our Masses. The organist was a very talented civilian who gave the congregation many years of service. I know she was aware that her work was appreciated. I just don't recall if I praised and thanked her sufficiently at one or more of our masses. She certainly deserved it.

I remember the first Sunday I offered Mass at the chapel. After it was completed, she and some members of her family invited me to breakfast at a local restaurant. Everyone ordered their breakfast and each of their orders included grits. Being from the far north, I never heard of grits. So when the waitress took my order I ordered bacon and eggs and did not include grits. The waitress had a puzzled look and asked if I wanted grits with my breakfast. I answered "I don't know what a grit is can I sample one." She said "certainly." While we waited, I had imagined she would return with a bun or a slice of some meat product. A minute or so later she returned to the table holding a fork and a piece of some little white thing on the end of one of the prongs. My surprise must have been visible immediately as I heard them laugh and the waitress ask again if I wanted grits with my breakfast. I ordered the grits; enjoyed it and in the future made it a part of my breakfast orders. Trying grits for the first time reminded me of a practice I had when travelling in foreign countries. I always eat the food native to the country. I don't recall ever being disappointed, with one exception. While we were anchored outside Taranto Italy, officers on the *Shangri-La* were invited by the Italian Navy Installation for dinner at their officer's club. The food was absolutely excellent. They served oysters as an appetizer. I had never eaten an oyster and was not all that impressed with the looks of this mollusk. Doc Race and I were sitting next to each other and at first we both hesitated to try them. Finally, we decided what possible harm could come from eating just one oyster. We each ate one and commented on the way it slid down our throats. Little did we know what could happen when eating one little oyster taken from the Mediterranean. This little monster took Doc and me out of service for at least three days. I seldom left the latrine without a return trip minutes later. Doc had the same experience but he spent his "up" time trying to discover a cure for our ailment. Eventually, Mother Nature worked out the problem and we returned to a normal life aboard ship.

There were two chaplains, a Catholic and a Protestant, assigned to the base. Both of our offices were located within the Ellyson Field chapel. Scheduling of time of religious services had been established many years before our service there. The times of Sunday services were the same as they are in almost every Navy station; Catholics offered Mass at 8:00 and 10:00 o'clock while Protestants held their services at 9:00 o'clock. The body of the church was a perfect fit for religious programs. As mentioned above, besides religious services, the chapel served as the facility for graduation ceremonies.

For the most part, Naval, Marine and some Air Force pilots graduating from our school, would be transferred overseas to serve in Vietnam. Some Coast Guard pilots were also assigned to Vietnam but they were frequently assigned to other billets such as serving on costal naval bases where they could respond rapidly to vessels and persons under distress. The thought on all of our minds was the dangers these men would face as they moved personnel and supplies into areas where the fighting was the most intense. Many of our helicopter pilots lost their lives or were seriously wounded during their tours in Vietnam, remnants of which they would carry with them for the rest of their lives. Everyone who joins the Armed Forces understands that giving their lives or being seriously injured is a real possibility. The loss of life among helicopter pilots and crew in combat was a relatively frequent experience. Records vary on figures concerning pilots and crew members killed during the Vietnam conflict. One of the more reliable figures shows 2,202 pilots and 2,704 crew members were killed and 5,086 helicopters were destroyed. Students involved in the training program were fully aware of the danger they would face and accepted it as a necessary element of their work. Graduation ceremonies carried a sense of apprehension as well as pride for the pilot and his parents, wife, and family members. On occasions like this, it became apparent that military service is a family affair. All of them, parents, children, relatives and friends participate fully whether in active service or at home and they all make huge sacrifices to protect and advance the best interests of this nation. All of them deserve the thanks and respect of the nation.

Chapter 19
End of My Tour as a Navy Chaplain

At the end of my tour at Ellyson Field I had completed eight years of active service, four with the US Marines and four with Naval Air. I cherish every day I was able to serve with the really great men and women in the Armed Forces and thank God for the quality of our service personnel. Equally deserving of our appreciation are the military families whose sacrifices were made generously and at time cost them dearly. Managing family life alone, ensuring the best interests of the children and living within a budget calls for careful spending decisions and the dozens of other responsibilities which weigh heavy on the folks back home. All of them single and married served the best interests of our nation by actively participating in the military and by supporting their efforts at home maintaining a stable home and a loving, productive family.

Looking Back At Eight Year Of Service

Reviewing the above discussions led me to evaluate the manner in which I carried out my priesthood as a member of the Armed Forces. From the day I entered the navy, I became fully absorbed in my work and spent as much time as I could with the troops on a base, or a ship or working closely with the families trying to bring Christ into their lives. My intention was to perform my priesthood where I believe Jesus spent his time on earth.

Jesus Was a Carpenter Working and Living in His Community

His entire life was a prayer but He did not spend all his time in the local synagogue. He lived his life working with Joseph as a carpenter making tables, chairs and home structures, farm equipment and other things needed by the community. This activity called for His presence at the work sites, listening to the client's wishes and devising approaches to carry out the contracts. Even in His public ministry, references were made to Jesus being the son of a carpenter, a member of Nazareth's middle-class families.

He had relatives and friends in the Nazareth community and was very much a part of their lives. When He was invited to attend a wedding feast at Cana, He went with His mother and probably some of his disciples. It would be no stretch of the imagination to believe Jesus took part in the wedding ceremonies, singing songs with the other guest and enjoying the food and wine set before the guests. It would seem unlikely that Jesus did not partake of the wine as it was the appropriate beverage for meals at home and at celebrations such as a wedding feast. During the festivities, the host ran out of wine and, Jesus, to avoid embarrassment to host, and at the direction of his mother, worked His first miracle by turning six jars of water into an extraordinarily excellent wine. This action, in response to his mother's concern, is ample demonstration that her petitions are accepted and thoroughly favored by her son, Jesus Christ.

Jesus was a close friend and associate of Lazarus and his sisters. When Lazarus died, Jesus reacted as anyone of us would at the news of the death of a dear friend. He was filled with emotion and cried. Then, given His divinity, he was able to correct the situation. He went with Mary and Martha, sisters of Lazarus, to the burial site and had the stone covering the tomb removed. The sisters advised Him the body of Lazarus was probably decaying, a less than attractive sight. Aware of this, He called into the tomb telling Lazarus to come out, which he did. This miracle clearly demonstrated his mastery over all creation. However, an important element of this occasion is Jesus did it out of love for His friends. He spent much of His time preaching to multitudes of people in the temple at Jerusalem, in the synagogues and wherever people would gather to listen to Him. He had a special love for children and the poor. He demonstrated His love by being with them, sharing their lives, demonstrating by His life that God cared for them and wanted to be a part of their lives. His disciples had a special mission. They were to carry on His teaching and by their example demonstrate how the faith preached by Jesus was to be lived. He spent three years with them, walking in the countryside, teaching the principles to govern their lives and those of his followers. He ate with them, fished with them and dealt with each of them as individuals. He was an active member of his community; living like other citizens, participating in the activities of His time and place. His life was lived with the people He came to save. He had enemies who feared Him, attacked Him and eventually killed Him. Knowing His teaching was aggravating the scribes and Pharisees, He did not hide in some cave or other place of safety. He stayed with his apostles and continued to bring God's truths to the crowds following Him wherever He went.

Of course this does not mean He never spent quiet time meditating and praying. The Scriptures tell us He would go off by Himself to spend intimate, private time with His father. He went to the synagogue to worship and showed all of us that every moment of our lives should be lived in prayer. Working with people was one important form of Christ's prayer life. At the end of His life, He received no acknowledgement for the dignity befitting His Person or even recognition of His love and the miraculous events that characterized His life. His good works were rewarded with a condemnation as a criminal taken off the streets and crucified, and in his case, between two thieves.

This is not to suggest an exact identity between the life of a chaplain and that of Our Lord. Rather, I believe Christ lived his life in the company of others and by His presence demonstrated God loved them and wanted to be with them. Christ lived his life and died for us for which we must always be grateful. In like manner, the sailor or Marine who meets a similar end protecting the citizens of this nation deserves our gratitude. The country is benefited by their service and the nations' future greatness is ensured by their participation in American life.

The chaplain lives his life with military personnel and their families, attempting to bring their lives into a relationship with God, recognizing their dependence on Him and His desire to bring them happiness here and in eternity. The chaplain's position is important as it recognizes military personnel like all other citizens have a spiritual side that requires attention and the opportunity to express their love for God through participation in religious services. Washington and the citizen founders of this nation realized it is not always easy to find

God in a life filled with combat struggles. But, in their time as in ours, we recognize that God is here with us as He is with those living a civilian life. This presence includes being with the men and women in the Armed Forces.

Jesus and the Centurion

The Gospel according to St. Luke recounts the occasion when a Roman soldier, a centurion, requested Jesus to use His power to cure his seriously ill servant. Feeling unworthy to make the request personally, he sent some elders of the Jews to request Jesus to come to the aid of his servant. When asked, Jesus responded immediately and went with the elders fully aware the request came from a soldier who believed Jesus had the power to cure the sick. The request of the elders included comments about their respect for the Centurion and his generosity by building their synagogue. Jesus went with them to heal the Centurion's servant. This event is worth quoting as it demonstrates both the faith and humility of the Centurion and the respect Jesus had for this man's expression of faith.

Luke 7:1-10:

"When Jesus had finished saying all this to the people who were listening, he entered Capernaum. There a centurion's servant, whom his master valued highly, was sick and about to die. The centurion heard of Jesus and sent some elders of the Jews to him, asking him to come and heal his servant. When they came to Jesus, they pleaded earnestly with him, "This man deserves to have you do this, because he loves our nation and has built our synagogue." So Jesus went with them. He was not far from the house when the centurion sent friends to say to him: "Lord, don't trouble yourself, for I do not deserve to have you come under my roof. That is why I did not even consider myself worthy to come to you. But say the word, and my servant will be healed. For I myself am a man under authority, with soldiers under me. I tell this one, 'Go,' and he goes; and that one, 'Come,' and he comes. I say to my servant, 'Do this,' and he does it." When Jesus heard this, he was amazed at him, and turning to the crowd following him, he said, "I tell you, I have not found such great faith even in Israel." Then the men who had been sent returned to the house and found the servant well."

Christ's acknowledgement of the Centurion's faith says a great deal about His willingness to acknowledge and respect the requests of those who serve in the military. Christ's spiritual life was expressed in the hours of solitude with his Father and continued in His associations with those He encountered in His daily life. The chaplain, ever aware of this relationship with God, spends his life in the military working with military personnel in all elements of their lives; healing personal wounds, often more painful than physical hurts, and helping them find God's directives in their daily lives.

Chapter 20
Final Thoughts

Having read and reread this book countless times and finally completing it, I became aware that many incidents I discussed concerned a tragedy of one sort or another.

When new recruits come on board, we are fully aware this new found behavioral freedom will cause some of them to become a problem to themselves and/or to the service. Dangers to their lives are not only related to combat situations. Remembering recruits are eighteen or nineteen years old and for the first time in their lives they are free of parental control and the social norms of the society they lived in, the independence they will now experience includes making value judgments without guidance from parents or teachers. Being a part of the indoctrination process as a chaplain, our objective was to remind them there is always a price to pay for such abuse and that the principles they learned while growing up still apply to them as they encounter adult life.

Those with a strong family background and an attachment to some religious affiliation are less often to become victims of drugs or alcohol abuse, although this is not true in every case. All of our experiences tell us people with those qualifications can submit to the same addictions. However, having been the chaplain of a brig in Okinawa, one factor became clear quickly. Marines and sailors who practiced their religion were not among the inmates. Participation in their faith keeps them in touch with moral principles that can guide their military and social lives. They encounter the same dangers as everyone else but their value systems kicks in when a determination is made whether or not to step over the line and begin a trip downhill. "God takes care of His own."

Today, our nation is experiencing an anti-Christian and in many cases an anti-God atmosphere and are replacing them with government controlled programs and leadership that finds morality totally without value. Our nation was founded as a republic. An observation made by John Adams speaks to a quality required of citizens to make it operate successfully;

> "Our Constitution was written for a religious and virtuous people; it will serve no other." It will not survive a society that lacks a sense of morality. Those of us, which include the great majority of Americans, believe in God, understand that justice and fairness rests with the application of God given principles to both personal and governmental actions."

A quotation from Edmund Burke's work "Revolution in France" speaks to the quality of citizens required for a republic to be successful:

> "Men are qualified for civil liberty in exact proportion to their disposition to put moral chains upon their own appetites,—in proportion as their love to justice is above their rapacity,— Society cannot exist, unless a controlling power upon will and appetite be placed somewhere; and the less of it there is within, the more there must be without. It is ordained in the eternal constitution of things, that men of intemperate minds cannot be free. Their passions forge their fetters."

EDMUND BURKE, "Letter to a Member of the National Assembly," 1791.The Works of the Right Honorable Edmund Burke, vol. 4, pp. 51–52 (1899).

The principles that formed the bedrock of our nation gave us unity of purpose and motivated our Continental Congress to create a republic based on the belief that the life of each individual has value and the capability to govern their lives, develop their talents, improve their state in life and be a constructive element in their society. To accomplish this, they had to be free of control by a foreign government, establish a government controlled by the citizens with the freedom established by the first amendment: "Congress shall make no law respecting an establishment of religion, or prohibiting the free exercise thereof; or abridging the freedom of speech, or of the press; or the right of the people peaceably to assemble, and to petition the government for a redress of grievances."

In the Revolutionary War, the military shouldered the load that freed our nation. Today, military personnel protect those same freedoms for the same reasons. I found respect for God and the free exercise of religion honored through every military command in which I served. I am and will continue to be grateful for the privilege of bringing God to the troops and the troops to God.

Raphael P Landreville.
Veteran, US Naval Chaplain

ABOUT THE AUTHOR

R aphael P. Landreville approached his chaplaincy as a mission to assist the troops to keep God in their lives although totally immersed in a world preparing to wage war. Ray was ordained in 1955 for the Diocese of Marquette, Michigan following years of study which included the Salvatorian Seminary, St. Nazianz, WI where he earned his AA. Ray continued his studies at St. Francis Major Seminary, Milwaukee, receiving his Bachelor's degree and completed his four years of studies in Theology at St. John Major Seminary, Plymouth, Michigan. After ordination to the priesthood he was assigned Assistant Pastor at St. Francis de Sales, Manistique, Michigan. The city was located on the shore of Lake Michigan surrounded by huge forests making it an extraordinarily excellent station for fishing, hunting and golfing when not engaged in parish work. After two years, he was transferred to St. Peter's Cathedral, Marquette, Michigan spending the next four years as an Assistant Pastor and Athletic Director. In both parishes he was an active member of the communities, teaching school directing school athletic programs organizing and managing youth groups and fulfilling his responsibilities to the parish community.

His father and brother served in the U.S. Army, his dad during WW I and his older brother served in the Far East during WWII. Their respect for their service encouraged him to do likewise but in the US Navy. Upon completion of the Chaplain Training Program in Newport, RI his first assignment was to the 5th Marines, Camp Pendleton, California where he participated in the Cuban Conflict, served in Okinawa, Japan and spent two years at the Maine Supply and Maintenance Base in Barstow, California. His next two years were served on the Aircraft Carrier USS *Shangri-La*, (CVA 38) touring the Mediterranean and two years at Ellyson Field Naval Air Station, Pensacola, Florida, the training base for helicopter pilots. He approached his chaplaincy as a mission to assist the troops to keep

God in their lives although totally immersed in a world preparing to wage war during the Vietnam conflict.

The commands in which he served were his parishes where he brought the Catholic faith to their daily lives through the Sacrifice of the Mass, daily and on Sundays, baptized family members and converts to the faith, ensured the children received the Sacrament of Confirmation and members were married. Funerals, although infrequent, were held at naval chapels. The chapel also served as a convenient location for instructing children preparing for their First Communion and Confirmation. Personal counseling absorbed a considerable amount of his time as issues on substance abuse, marriage and financial difficulties and other circumstances impacted the daily lives of the military and of their families. Ultimately, his priestly life in the military was that of a priest in military uniform.

After completing an eight year tour, he returned to civilian life, grateful for the opportunity to bring God to the troops and the troops to God.